Graham Warman and Paul Sorrell

PENGUIN BOOKS

Published by the Penguin Group
Penguin Group (NZ), 67 Apollo Drive, Rosedale,
North Shore 0632, New Zealand (a division of Pearson New Zealand Ltd)
Penguin Group (USA) Inc., 375 Hudson Street,
New York, New York 10014, USA
Penguin Group (Canada), 90 Eglinton Avenue East, Suite 700, Toronto,
Ontario, M4P 2Y3, Canada (a division of Pearson Penguin Canada Inc.)
Penguin Books Ltd, 80 Strand, London, WC2R 0RL, England
Penguin Ireland, 25 St Stephen's Green,
Dublin 2, Ireland (a division of Penguin Books Ltd)
Penguin Group (Australia), 250 Camberwell Road, Camberwell,
Victoria 3124, Australia (a division of Pearson Australia Group Pty Ltd)
Penguin Books India Pvt Ltd, 11, Community Centre,
Panchsheel Park, New Delhi – 110 017, India
Penguin Books (South Africa) (Pty) Ltd, 24 Sturdee Avenue,
Rosebank, Johannesburg 2196, South Africa

Penguin Books Ltd, Registered Offices: 80 Strand, London, WC2R 0RL, England

First published by Penguin Group (NZ), 2008
5 7 9 10 8 6

Commissioning Editor Alison Brook
Managing Editor Andrea Coppock

Designed and typeset by Seven
Prepress by Image Centre Ltd
Printed by Everbest Printing Co. Ltd, China

ISBN: 978 0 14 300860 6

A catalogue record for this book is available
from the National Library of New Zealand.

www.penguin.co.nz

Catch of the day

contents

foreword

I met the fabulous Fleur, a legend in her own lifetime, in 1995 when I filmed her for *Taste NZ*. She then owned Olivers in Clyde and fed me rabbit, venison and pickled walnut pie, which we called bunny and bambi pie. This was her look – cowboy boots with silver Harley Davidson tips, crushed velvet and big blond hair-do. She's a South Islander through and through, and therefore well ahead in the hospitality, likeability and personality department. Fleur is a woman who does not believe in mixing anything and everything on a plate to give the impression of innovation at any price. Hers is a cuisine of generosity, respect and sensitivity. She works by instinct, knowledge and feeling, rather than technical wizardry. If you asked her for a mushroom, she would give you a whole feast; if you asked her for a piece of cheese she would give you a platter; if you asked her the time of day she would tell you a story. Fleur is a no equipment, no show-off, no fuss cook. The hands-down secret is in her ingredients – the freshest tomatoes, the best oil, the flippiest fish, the nuttiest Maori potatoes. She and her cooks use ingredients most of us walk past – seaweed, puffballs, hedgerow berries, wild mushrooms and horopito leaves. I hope you enjoy Fleur's no-nonsense, sunny approach to life and good cooking.

Peta Mathias
May 2008

acknowledgements

When in early 2007 photographer Graham Warman suggested that we collaborate on a book on Fleurs Place at Moeraki, I saw in an instant that this was an idea whose time had come. English media chef Rick Stein's visit to the restaurant in October 2006 had sown the seed of an idea in Graham's mind — why shouldn't the South's own celebrity restaurateur have her own cookbook? What was good enough for Rick, Peta and Stephanie was certainly good enough for Fleur.

Fleur Sullivan's new restaurant in coastal North Otago had rapidly built a national - and international - reputation, and a book combining her recipes with a portrait of the area as a 'regional food study', involving people, places, landscape and wildlife, was bound to attract widespread interest. Given the restaurant's location in a wild and beautiful natural setting, we adopted a seasonal structure for the book - both as a way of apportioning the recipes and introducing readers to the many facets of Moeraki that have gone into making Fleurs Place the remarkable phenomenon it has become in a few short years.

Fleur opened her heart to the book and right from the start gave us every help and encouragement. Our primary debt of gratitude is to this remarkable and far-sighted woman. Simon Peacock, her head chef, generously opened his recipe book and responded to our never-ending stream of requests and enquiries. I recall numerous occasions on which Simon would produce dish after flawlessly presented dish, which Graham would photograph and which we would then sample, accompanied by eye-rolling and ecstatic groans ... And we had the cheek to call it work!

We are grateful, too, to Fleur's kitchen and waiting staff who always made room for us, even at their busiest times, and went out of their way to be friendly and helpful. Without their willing and enthusiastic co-operation our job would have been nothing like the fun it nearly always was. Fleur's growers and suppliers were also unfailingly helpful and co-operative, and we are especially grateful to Alison and Dugald McTavish, who showed us great warmth and hospitality on several visits to their Moeraki property and opened our eyes to the endless possibilities of vegetable gardening.

One of our deepest debts of gratitude is to Penguin Books, who immediately saw the merit of our

proposal and took a big punt on a couple of Southern lads who are not exactly household names. We only hope we have fulfilled the promise they saw in us. We are especially grateful to our publisher, Alison Brook, who guided us along each step of the way and prodded us gently when we needed it and to our managing editor, Andrea Coppock, who handled the difficult task of assembling the finished product with cheerful efficiency. The layout and design work by Gideon Keith of Seven has brilliantly realised our vision for the look and feel of the book.

Thanks are due as well to the staff of the Heritage Collections at the Dunedin Public Libraries, for their ever courteous and timely service, and to Professor Richard Norris of the University of Otago Geology Department, for supplying details about the geology of Moeraki.

Paul Sorrell
Graham Warman
May 2008

SLOW
DOWN

introduction

Every time I visit Moeraki I'm surprised I don't have to take a boat or a plane to get there. On the contrary, the visitor only needs to drive up State Highway 1 for an hour from Dunedin, turn right at the boat-sitting-in-a-field (the *Lee Anne*), and take the short access road that brings you to the village nestled on the seaward edge of the stubby peninsula. Somehow it should be more difficult. I think it's because going to Moeraki is like visiting an island, a place remote from the cares of city life, where the pace slows down, people stop to chat and you can feel the tension of urban living drain away from the moment you arrive. The name itself – 'sleepy sky' or 'a place to sleep by day' – captures the essence of the Moeraki experience.

The Haberfield family headstone in the urupa at Second Kaik.

A boatshed crib sits hard up against the shoreline at First Kaik.

Like anywhere worth seeing, the best way to introduce yourself to Moeraki is on foot. Stop at the sign that says 'Millennium Walkway' and walk a few yards to the start of the track. Look left and you'll see a magnificent arc of unbroken sands sweeping away to low, distant hills. The tiny dots about 1.8 km away, just visible to the naked eye, are the fabled Moeraki Boulders, spectacular spherical concretions that have eroded out of the mudstone slopes behind the beach. The larger examples measure up to 2.2 m across and may have taken 4 to 5.5 million years to form. Ngai Tahu tradition has a more imaginative explanation. According to legend, the Araiteuru canoe, carrying colonists from the central Pacific, was wrecked in a storm at Matakaea (Shag Point) and its contents strewn along the neighbouring coastline. The round food baskets, gourds and seed kumara it was carrying became Te Kaihinaki (the Moeraki Boulders) and other boulders further south at Katiki Beach (known locally as Katigi).

Carry on towards the village as the track passes through dense tunnels of foliage, native and introduced woven together. On a warm day in late spring, the air is heavy with the sweet smell of lupins and alive with birdsong. Shelves of eroded mudstone and volcanic rock fringed by coarse quartz sands of a striking orange hue – used as a pebble-dash cladding on Dunedin's stately home 'Olveston' – are given over to fossicking black oystercatchers and rowdy red-billed gulls. A scattering of dwellings marks the approach to the village and a dozen boats are resting at anchor in the bay.

On the headland above the village, the track ends at the Whalers' Lookout, offering spectacular views of the coast from Cape Wanbrow near Oamaru to the Otago Heads in the south, with endless tracts of ocean between. History is close here. And so is community. A plaque erected to commemorate Moeraki's founding as a Pakeha whaling settlement, on Boxing Day 1836, is twinned with another which reads: 'This monument, erected for the 150th anniversary of Moeraki, December 26th 1986, honours Maori and Pakeha descendants, families and associates of this area'. Not far below, an old pa site is occupied by a helicopter pad, catering for those who feel that they really *do* need to take the journey by air.

Other parts of the peninsula are best visited by car. Near the village, past the tavern, motor camp and holiday cottages to rent, sit the marae and the school, founded in 1890, closed in 1989 and now the administration offices for Te Runanga o Moeraki. A couple of roads branch out from the village, winding through hilly pastureland, interspersed with scrub and macrocarpa, clumps of pine and the odd farmhouse. One leads to the tiny beachside collection of fibrolite and weatherboard cribs known as First Kaik (for kaika, 'village').

The other road leads to the lighthouse and wildlife reserve at Katigi Point, the furthest point from the village, but no visitor should miss the turn-off to Second Kaik, a second crib hamlet hugging the shores of a beautiful little bay ornamented with spreading shelves of volcanic rock, orange sands and beds of swirling kelp. I have never seen such a rich palette of seaweeds, festooning the rocks and swirling up along the shoreline. A couple of herons fly lazily over the beach and a few fur seals sprawl over the bigger rock stacks to the right. It takes a moment to spot them, as they are the same colour as the rocks. Looking towards First Kaik, you can see the big rock stack of Maukiekie Island covered with ranks of nesting shags of three species – little, spotted and New Zealand's northernmost colony of Stewart Island shags. As I drove in, I could see a huge black sea lion relaxing in the rocky shallows. It had gone by the time I got down to the beach – but I almost fell over a smaller animal imitating a heap of brown kelp on the sand. This is the way New Zealand must have looked a long time ago.

If nature is here in abundance, so is history. The urupa behind the settlement is like an open book. Although many of the headstones are worn and weathered, they tell the story of the fusion of Maori and Pakeha, wresting a hard living from land and sea in this corner of coastal Otago. One commemorates Ritea, the wife of pioneer whaler William Haberfield, 'who met her sad death in the Port Chalmers fire, July 7th 1907, aged 25 years, also her son Tahu Puriri Teaika,

aged 4 years. Also of Hine Afitea Kathleen Rehu who died in the Dunedin Hospital from the effects of burns, aged 12 years'.

Get back onto Kaika Road and it will take you to Moeraki's furthest outpost, Katigi Point, the site of an early Maori village and fortified pa established in the eighteenth century by the feuding chief Taoka. Built on a long tongue of land snaking down to the sea, the pa was protected by a narrow neck defended by terraces, trenches and palisades. While this early settlement has left few traces on the landscape (although the terracing is clearly visible from the air), the point is dominated by an imposing wooden lighthouse built in 1878 and still in service, although the last resident keeper was withdrawn in 1975.

But the real drawcard of this slim peninsula that slopes steeply down to the tiny island at its tip is the wildlife. Yellow-eyed and little blue penguins, fur seals and shags are all abundant here. Seals bask and fight in the rockpools below the cliffs and, in the late afternoons, the yellow-eyed penguins begin coming ashore, surfing up on the red-sand beaches and climbing the grassy slopes to their nest sites. Featuring in popular tour guides such as *Fodor's*, Katigi Point has become a drawcard for visitors from all over the world. In the penguin-viewing hide, positioned so as to show off a slice of impossibly pristine beach, cameras and binoculars are trained at the ready and German is the language of the day. Resting comically on their bellies at the edge of the bush or wandering in groups along steep grassy slopes, these rare yellow-eyes are more approachable here than anywhere in the world.

Fleur's Story

When Fleur Sullivan arrived in this special place in 1997, she had no intention of setting up a restaurant. She would have been more than happy to end her days at Olivers Restaurant and lodge in Clyde, where she had built a reputation through the 1980s and '90s as a restaurateur dedicated to serving top-quality locally produced food and wines. But after being diagnosed with cancer, she sold Olivers to enable her to take best advantage of her course of chemotherapy for 12 months. 'I always knew that at some stage I would live in Moeraki – possibly when I was 102', recalls Fleur. It also meant that she was nearer her mother in Oamaru.

Having found and settled into her house on the windswept headland above the village, Fleur turned to her surroundings to occupy her time. Trips on local fishing boats had opened her eyes to the variety and quality of the local kaimoana, and she could see that the fish-parts discarded by the fishermen – 'all those beautiful heads and frames, wings and livers' – would make wonderful stock and soup. Inspired by this romantic notion, she purchased a catering caravan and hawker's licence and set up on the old wharf, selling fresh and smoked fish, bread and soup to passers-by.

Word began to spread – fast – culminating in an interview with radio host Kim Hill and a mention on Jim Hickey's weather report on TV1, after which everyone in New Zealand knew where Fleur was. She had never given up the habit of collecting cutlery, crockery and furniture and had storage sheds full of second-hand doors and windows back in Clyde. Despite

A moulting yellow-eyed penguin in the reserve at Katagi Point.

sporting a badge given to her by Peta Mathias that proclaimed 'If I look like I'm buying another restaurant, shoot me!', Fleur discovered the perfect site down at the old jetty with a 'For sale' sign attached. The final piece in the puzzle came to hand when she bought a tumbledown shed that was languishing as a railway siding in Maheno.

Dilapidated though it was, it provided the roof beams and flooring timbers for the restaurant that was now rapidly taking shape. Local builders Rudie Verhoef and Mark Bonar, friends of Fleur's children, were sympathetic to the project and realised Fleur's vision.

If the building evolved at its own pace, so did its fittings. Fleur is the first to admit that she is a natural recycler and as a result the restaurant is filled with furnishings and fittings that all tell a story. The elegant wooden staircase was salvaged from the demolition of the Hudson family mansion in Dunedin, the walls are hung with old maps and maritime prints and a large window seat is fashioned out of the hull of a wrecked Moeraki fishing boat. An old Shacklock range heats the place in winter, and the tables and chairs were salvaged from under the grandstand at the Oamaru racecourse. An elaborate sculpture, commissioned from artist Andy Ducker, holds wine glasses above the bar. History is important to Fleur and her knowledge and sense of style have been called on to assist with television and film projects shot in the Central Otago region. 'In another life I would have been a film set designer.'

The creation of the restaurant witnessed the forager in Fleur, which is also reflected in her approach to food. When she first arrived in Moeraki, she delighted in scouring the hills for puffballs, field mushrooms and ink-caps and seeking out wild delicacies such as native spinach, wild parsley, mint, watercress and Maori potatoes. Puha and mussels could be gathered to make a simple yet delicious dish. She tried out the abundant local seaweeds as ingredients in soup and began experimenting with drying eels in the open air and smoking cod heads in a home-made smoker.

The notion of garnering food from one's surroundings, living without want or waste, was deeply engrained in Fleur from her childhood. She grew up in the midst of a large extended family on a farm established by her great-grandparents at Tawai near the Waitaki River. Here the family maintained a big vegetable garden and Fleur collected field mushrooms in the paddocks and tickled trout in the streams. She remembers her father as a hunter, a dedicated fisherman who would shoot rabbits from the running board of the family car with his daughter at the wheel. Preserving was mostly left to the Great Aunts while her mother would make the family soap – 'she loved beautiful things'.

When asked about her philosophy of food, Fleur will tell you that she was unknowingly an advocate of 'slow food' long before the term became fashionable. 'I just call it good food. Naturally good food.' It's the kind of food our grandparents took for granted and that we have lost the art of preparing. It's about having respect for food and those who produce it, and respect too for the enjoyment of a shared table. The slow

Maukiekie Island is topped with colonies of three species of shag.

food movement is about reclaiming these lost gastronomic traditions, and she is scathing about the harm done to us and our food by globalised agribusiness and the 'McDonalds culture' it has spawned. Fleur uses the restaurant to rediscover and promote heritage produce like Maori potatoes and organic tomatoes and knows the location of every old apple and quince tree in the district.

Fleur is clear that any food she serves needs to have three characteristics: it must be fresh, honest and locally produced.

What guarantees the freshness of Fleur's fish is her location. Because Moeraki is a 'day port', the handful of boats still working the inshore fishery are able to land their catch daily. This is the reason the restaurant exists.

As a licensed fish receiver, Fleur is able to buy off the local fishermen who own their own quota and are willing to do the extra paperwork involved. She also has her own quota of fish which is caught by local fisherman Gavin Te Maiharoa, who also supplies most of the fish for the restaurant. Fleur is closely involved in the selection and landing of her fish and, when she can, relishes the ritual of going over to inspect Gavin's catch when he ties up at the wharf. Later, the catch she has ordered is ferried across the bay by dinghy and winched right up to the restaurant on an old trolley system.

The notion of freshness is best illustrated by her approach to fish. A typical menu lists blue cod, tarakihi, groper, gurnard, moki, ling and whole flatfish. The menu is based on fresh fish that is cooked quickly and simply, hand-filleted at sea and washed only in salt water by way of preparation and served with a choice of four simple sauces and the freshest steamed vegetables.

Presenting the food honestly and with integrity presents its own challenges. 'There's only so many things that you can do with a menu.' And there are no shortcuts: 'everything starts from scratch'. Fleur invites us to consider the lengthy process by which her 'naturally good food' finds its way onto the diner's plate. 'We start from the seed, whether planted by nature or by the grower, or the fish in the ocean. By the time it's presented at the kitchen door, inspected by the head and sous chef, passed on to the apprentices and commis chefs in the prep kitchen, then plated, sauced and garnished and handed to the wait staff, you are looking at a veritable diamond sitting on your plate.'

The sense of locality, of region, is of paramount importance to Fleur. The building she has created looks as if it has 'always been there' and would not have been out of place in the old whaling days. After all, she says, 'I'm right where they pulled the whales up'. For one of Fleur's principal suppliers, Roger Belton of Southern Clams, Fleur's genius lies in her successful combination of a sense of style with a feeling for place. By integrating Moeraki's whaling past into her culinary vision, and maintaining respect for the place and its people, Fleur has created something that is far removed from the deracinated world of international cuisine with its predictable food and Legoland architecture. As Belton notes, 'integrating food with being there' is something that southern Europeans in particular have always known about.

From her early days in Central Otago, Fleur was a pioneer with what can be done with New Zealand products in general and regional cuisine in particular. She was an advocate of regional food long before it became popular and had the imagination to see how it can be integrated with other aspects of locale, such as tourism and local history, and utilised to set the ambience for a restaurant. In Clyde, she restored Olivers as a heritage setting in which to serve local food and fledgling Central Otago wines, and set up the Otago Goldfields' Heritage Trust and the Dunstan Cavalcade as ways of preserving and promoting the historical character of the region – and bringing it into the present.

But if Fleur is a pioneer, she has not worked alone. While she only employs people who are sympathetic to her philosophy, she stresses that it can be 'a battle to get the people I'm working with to fully understand why we work the way we do'. Along with the proponents of the slow food movement, she relishes the rituals and culture around food and appreciates the importance of the links between producers, purveyors and consumers that hold the 'food chain' together.

Fleurs Place is one node on a web that stretches across the lower South Island and includes growers and suppliers like Roger Belton, Alison McTavish from Moeraki, Kaan's Catering Supplies in Dunedin, Joe's Vegetables at Totara and Whitestone Cheese in Oamaru – and, of course, the people who flock to Moeraki from all over the world to dine at her table. Despite the difficulties, Fleur says that she has had little trouble attracting like-minded people to become part of her venture at Moeraki. 'It's like dropping a little stone in a pond because people come here and enjoy good food, fresh food, and then the word gets out to suppliers, growing something special, with different produce coming on at different times...' That small stone has set off a sequence of ripples that are unlikely to fade away anytime soon.

Paul Sorrell, May 2008

A weatherboard crib at First Kaik.

autumn

01/

Fleur Sullivan is very much a hands-on host. The first thing visitors see as they round the bar is her unmistakable figure seated at a simple wooden desk piled high with paperwork – some of which will eventually get attended to. Being sequestered away in a backroom office would be anathema to her. Here she can interact freely with her cooking and waiting staff, greet customers, play with her grandchildren and pass the time of day with anyone who wants to chat. Fleur forms the hub of a lively world of chatter, gossip, laughter and good food that constantly swirls around her.

Slow food

Simple. Good. Honest. Fresh. Local. These are some of the terms Fleur uses to describe the food she serves at Fleurs Place. And people have responded by flocking here in droves. She says that she was part of the 'slow food' movement before it became fashionable. To her, it is simply a question of reclaiming a culinary tradition that is still within the reach of living memory. She remembers a time not so long

fleurs Place
open 7 days for
naturally good
food = off the Boats
tonight = FLAT FISH

Gavin Te Maiharoa's boat, *Matai*, approaches the fisherman's wharf at Moeraki with the catch of the day.

CHARTERS

Fleur gathers bull kelp from the beach at First Kaik for her kelp and shellfish dish (see page 165).

ago when 'we all had a garden, and your granddad or your dad left a couple of plants at the end of the row to go to seed, so you saved the best' – a time when people knew how to cook barley and lentils, and added dried pasta to a pot of boiling water rather than reaching for the instant noodles.

Fleur as forager

If the restaurant took its shape from Fleur's activities as a collector and recycler of second-hand building materials and furnishings, it continues to benefit from her ongoing role as a forager of wild foods. From her first days in Moeraki, searching for puffballs and Maori potatoes growing on waste ground at the edges of the village, Fleur has progressed to collecting an assortment of wild fungi in season – shaggy ink-caps, field mushrooms, slippery jack (a bolete) and (rather mysteriously) 'lots of little ones'. Anything potentially dodgy is referred to Crop and Food Research in Dunedin for identification.

Although Fleur grows a variety of herbs in her own garden to supply the restaurant, she is not above the occasional foraging trip in a neighbour's vegetable patch.

Seaweed

Surrounded on almost all sides by ocean beaches, seaweed is something Fleur is hardly able to avoid. Yet seaweed had always played a small part in her life – she talks of carrageen, Bonnington's Irish Moss, seaweed custard and laver bread, traditional uses of abundant natural products that our grandmothers kept alive but are now in danger of dying out. She's also learned something of Maori ways with seaweeds, especially from coastal dwellers in the North Island, and is keen to put in a plug for the Portobello Aquarium on Otago Peninsula – 'the perfect place to go and find out what you can and can't eat'.

Fleur uses seaweed in a variety of ways – as an ingredient in cooking, and as a garnish and flavour-enhancer on fish dishes. For example, she collects Japanese wakame and dries it for use as a condiment, or smokes it and sprinkles it on salmon. She also harvests sea lettuce – but only when it has floated free of the rocks – and uses it as a garnish on the kaimoana platter, where it complements the dish beautifully. The karengo used in the dumplings served with Simon's Irish lamb stew is closely related to Japanese nori and was a traditional delicacy for Maori.

Fleur also collects the bull kelp that southern Maori traditionally used as containers to preserve muttonbirds harvested from the titi islands around Rakiura (Stewart Island). Fleur uses its broad pouches to encase an impressive-looking dish of steamed clams and mussels, and enjoys a trip down to the beach at First Kaik to pull her quarry ashore. Once back at the restaurant, keeping it fresh is essential: 'I'll tie it to my jetty so that I can go down and slice a piece off. You have to keep your seaweed fresh.'

Blessed by a whale

A southern right whale visited Fleurs Place in its very early days, swimming up and down within metres of the shoreline. Fleur strongly believes that the great creature blessed the restaurant and took its destiny out of her hands. Its visit formed a link with Moeraki's whaling past and offered a good omen for the future. 'It'd been a long long time since a whale had been this close in the bay and that made me feel good … it made me feel that I'd done things right. And when I started to have some hassles with the local council, one of the dear old men from the village said, "You leave that girl alone, that whale is the father of a kaumatua from the first kaik and it appears to very few people." That made me feel really special, too.'

autumn recipes

'I enjoyed learning traditional recipes like this from my friend Paaka who had the time to show me how to find puha and where to gather the best and biggest mussels from the rocks on the Katigi Strait between Moeraki and Shag Point.'

makes one small jar

Toroi

ingredients

3 dozen mussels, fresh and cleaned
2 large handfuls of puha or watercress
250 ml (approximately) of your favourite vinegar (malt, white wine, cider, etc.)

method

1 Take care in shucking the fresh mussels from the shells, removing the beards and checking for any small crabs.
2 Chop the raw mussel meat coarsely.
3 Rub the puha in your hands to remove the bitterness, rinse and pat dry with paper towels.
4 Chop and mix with the mussel meat.
5 Pack into a clean and sterilised preserving jar and fill to cover with the vinegar. Refrigerate and allow to marinate for a couple of hours before enjoying with fresh bread and the company of good friends.

'When Rick Stein was here I gave him one of former chef Gilbert Prevost's perfect duck-liver parfaits, along with our muttonbird dish. Rick had asked for our mussels and blue cod to follow the muttonbird, but I couldn't resist the temptation to produce a feast of our New Zealand cuisine.'

makes one standard terrine dish

Duck-liver Parfait

method

1 Preheat oven to 130 °C.
2 Wash and drain duck livers and discard the milk. Melt butter and keep warm.
3 Add the onion, garlic, herbs and peppercorns to the alcohol and simmer over moderate heat until nearly thick and syrupy.
4 Purée the duck livers until smooth.
5 Add the reduced alcohol and onion mixture and process with the eggs.
6 Add salt and finally the warm melted butter and process until well puréed and fine.
7 Pass through a fine sieve and pour into a greased, ceramic terrine dish and cover with the lid.
8 Place the terrine into a tray of warm water or bain-marie and cook for one hour or until a skewer comes out clean and is hot on the lips.
9 Allow to cool in the terrine dish and refrigerate overnight. Turn out by submerging the sides of the terrine in warm water.

Serve slices with crisp toast, a few pickled onions and cornichons and chutney of your choice.

ingredients

500 g fresh duck livers, sinews removed and soaked in milk overnight
500 g butter, melted
1 small onion, chopped
2 cloves garlic, crushed
Central Otago thyme
2 bay leaves
6 peppercorns
250 ml brandy, port or Madeira
5 eggs
2 tsp salt

'There are a lot of memories associated with muttonbird. It isn't often served in restaurants and it's always an honour when people tell me this is the best muttonbird dish they've had. My best memory of muttonbird was the dish prepared for me by Julian McKay in Invercargill – I remember it was drenched with watercress. I've also enjoyed learning how to gut and prepare a fresh bird.'

serves two

Muttonbird with Maori Potatoes & Spinach

ingredients

- 2 salted muttonbirds
- 10 small Maori potatoes such as the Moeraki potato or pawhero
- 2 handfuls of native New Zealand spinach, washed
- spinach oil (see below)

Spinach oil

- 1 bunch spinach, washed
- 1 bunch sorrel leaves, washed
- 100 ml sesame oil
- 500 ml olive oil
- 1 lemon, juiced
- salt and pepper

method

1 In a large pot, place the muttonbirds and cover with cold water.
2 Slowly bring to the boil and allow to simmer for a couple of minutes.
3 Taste the water; if it appears overly salty then drain, refill with fresh cold water and repeat the process. If not, continue to simmer until the leg bone just begins to give away from the flesh.
4 Remove from water and allow to cool.
5 Boil the potatoes until just tender. Place these in a roasting pan and place the boiled muttonbird on top.
6 Grill or roast on a high heat until the skin begins to crisp and the potatoes roast in the muttonbird fat.
7 Soften the spinach in the remaining fat just before serving and serve with spinach oil.

Spinach oil

In a food processor, place the spinach and sorrel and purée until smooth. Drizzle in both oils, then squeeze in lemon juice and season. Pass through a fine sieve.

'Local girl Missy Hollows, returned from cooking for the rich and famous overseas, devised this recipe while working at Fleurs Place. It has now become a permanent item on the menu and is regarded as one of the restaurant's "signature dishes".'

serves two

Bacon-wrapped Cod with Littleneck Clams

method

1 Preheat oven to 180 °C.

2 Lay two cod fillets together for each portion and wrap two slices of streaky bacon around the centres.

3 Place the two portions of bacon-wrapped cod fillets in an ovenproof frying-pan and drizzle with olive oil. Select a pan that fits the portions snugly.

4 Roast in hot oven until the bacon begins to crisp and the cod is almost cooked.

5 Remove from the oven to the stove-top and, on a moderate heat, deglaze (lift the flavours from the bottom of the pan) with the white wine while the cod is still in the pan.

6 Allow to boil, then add the cream. (This should come halfway up the cod fillets.)

7 Add clams.

8 Boil gently until the sauce begins to thicken slightly and the clams open, then add chopped herbs, ground black pepper and salt (but only if needed on tasting).

Serve with steamed seasonal vegetables and freshly dug new-season potatoes.

ingredients

- 4 small fillets blue cod, skin and bones removed
- 4 rashers streaky bacon or smoked pork belly
- 25 ml olive oil
- 100 ml white wine
- 150 ml cream
- 10 New Zealand littleneck clams, washed
- chopped garden herbs including parsley, chives, chervil, etc.

'Two years ago we bought a steamer oven – however did we manage without it? I'm always searching for the old, original fish steamers – and can still visualise very clearly the one I couldn't afford 25 years ago.'

serves two to three

Steamed Tarakihi with Oyster Mushrooms, Spring Onions & Ginger

ingredients

- 1 whole tarakihi, gutted, wings clipped, scaled and washed
- 4 oyster mushrooms, sliced
- 2 spring onions, whites and greens separated and sliced
- 1 clove garlic, sliced thinly
- 1-cm piece ginger, cut in thin strips
- 1 red chilli, sliced
- 1 tbsp sesame oil
- 1 tbsp fish sauce
- 1 tbsp sweet sherry
- 1 lime, juiced
- fresh coriander
- 2 tbsp kejap manis (Malaysian sweet soy)

method

1 Slash the tarakihi 3 times on both sides and place in a flat dish, able to fit in a steamer.

2 Arrange sliced mushrooms, spring onion, garlic, ginger and chilli on top of the fish and dress with sesame oil, fish sauce and sweet sherry.

3 Steam for around 12–15 minutes and transfer to a large serving platter. Rearrange cooked vegetables and herbs back over fish, pour over collected juices from the pan and finish with lime juice, fresh coriander and a drizzle of kejap manis.

A slice of the Moeraki coastline looking towards the lighthouse at Katigi Point.

'People's faces always light up when you put a dish of mussels down in front of them. Some folk regularly drive for miles just to eat our mussels – and they go home feeling healthy and revived. My friend Henrietta comes all the way from Morven.'

serves two

Steamed Mussels with White Wine, Garlic & Cream

ingredients

- 1 tbsp butter
- 1/2 onion, finely chopped
- 2 cloves garlic, finely minced
- 100 ml dry white wine
- 2 dozen mussels, washed and debearded
- 200 ml cream
- 1 good handful of fresh herbs, chopped (parsley, chives, chervil, etc.)

method

1 In a heavy-bottomed pot melt the butter and sweat the onion and garlic until translucent.

2 Add the white wine and allow to boil.

3 Drop in the mussels and cover with the lid of the pot. Steam gently until the mussels just begin to open.

4 Remove the lid, add the cream and simmer for a couple of minutes to finish the cooking.

5 Lastly, add chopped herbs with plenty of fresh cracked pepper.

'Rhubarb has been handed over the fence for generations. Lesley Hale from Hampden makes a great rhubarb chutney.'

serves six

Vanilla Pannacotta & Ginger-poached Rhubarb

ingredients

Pannacotta

3 leaves gelatine
1 litre cream
150 g sugar
1 vanilla pod, split

Ginger-poached rhubarb

200 g caster sugar
250 ml water
100 ml ginger wine
2 cm fresh ginger root, sliced
1 cinnamon stick
3 star anise
1 vanilla pod, split
1 kg rhubarb stalks, cut into batons

method

Pannacotta

1 Soften gelatine in cold water.
2 In a heavy-bottomed pan, heat cream to just below boiling point with the sugar and vanilla. Stir through softened gelatine leaves and allow to cool.
3 Strain through a fine sieve and pour into serving glasses or pottles for turning out.
4 Refrigerate and allow to set.

Ginger-poached rhubarb

1 In a wide tray or pan that fits on the stove-top, place all the ingredients except the rhubarb and bring to a gentle boil.
2 Turn the heat to the lowest setting and add the rhubarb so that it lies in one layer in the syrup. Cover with baking parchment and poach gently until just beginning to soften.
3 Place tray on cooling rack and allow the rhubarb to cool in the syrup.

Serve with the pannacotta along with shortbread biscuits or biscotti.

'The name of this dessert entices you to order it even if you are replete! Cherry-pitting beats scraping mussels any time.'

serves eight

Chocolate Fondants with Cherries & Tamarind Syrup

ingredients

200 g dark chocolate
200 g butter
4 eggs
160 g caster sugar
160 g plain flour
6 g baking powder
melted butter and cocoa for dusting moulds
16 pitted cherries

Tamarind syrup

500 ml water
300 g caster sugar
200 g tamarind paste rehydrated with 200 ml water

method

1 Preheat oven to 200 °C.
2 Over a double boiler, melt the chocolate and butter until smooth. Remove from heat.
3 Whisk together eggs and sugar, add to chocolate mixture and add dry ingredients.
4 Grease 8 individual pudding ramekins with butter and dust with cocoa. Divide mixture evenly and dot 2 cherries into the centre of each.
5 Bake for 12 minutes or until well risen and cooked around the edge, but still soft and molten in the centre.
6 Serve with your favourite ice cream and the tamarind syrup.

Syrup

1 Make a sugar syrup with the 500 ml water and sugar and pour over rehydrated tamarind paste.
2 Sieve through a fine strainer and keep warm.

makes 1 litre

Cardamom & Orange Ice Cream

ingredients

- 5 cardamom pods, seeds crushed
- 175 g caster sugar
- 125 ml water
- 4 eggs
- 125 ml concentrated orange juice (or 375 ml regular juice reduced by a third)
- 300 ml cream

method

1 Bring crushed cardamom seeds, sugar and water to the boil while stirring to dissolve the sugar.

2 Lightly beat eggs in an electric mixer.

3 Pour hot syrup over eggs while beating and allow to cool.

4 Stir through orange juice and cream, then churn in an ice-cream maker according to the manufacturer's instructions.

makes 1.3 litres

Vanilla Ice Cream

method

1 Combine the milk and cream with the split and scraped vanilla pods and gently bring to the boil.

2 Beat together the yolks and the sugars until thick and pale.

3 Pour the hot cream onto the yolks and return to the heat and cook only until it coats the back of a spoon.

4 Allow to cool, sieve, then churn in an ice-cream maker according to the manufacturer's instructions.

ingredients

540 ml milk
540 ml cream
2 vanilla pods
7 egg yolks
180 g caster sugar
180 g liquid glucose

'Bob and Sue are dedicated muttonbird enthusiasts. Their son Simon has inherited the same gene.'

Whitestone Cheese Board

Just as wine and cheese go together, Fleur's relationship with Whitestone Cheese, which goes back to her early days in Clyde, has followed a similar path to her connections with some of Central Otago's early winemakers. Their early farmhouse cheese was never missing from the breakfast room table at Olivers. And there was always a big jar of Whitestone feta in the Lodge kitchen – to be spread onto crackers for a late-night snack.

The Berry family, who own the company, make regular stops at Moeraki to resupply Fleur's cheese boards. Names like Mt Domet Double Cream brie, Livingstone Gold and Fuchsia Creek feta are redolent of the open North Otago landscape where these cheeses find their origins. The restaurant takes all their 20 or so cheeses including Windsor Blue, a special favourite as befits the country's most awarded cheese. Whitestone even make a Moeraki Bay Blue cheese in honour of the longstanding relationship.

Fleur recalls how she and founders Bob and Sue Berry have enjoyed one another's company over many years and continue to appear together at the increasingly popular Oamaru Wine and Food Festival which takes place on the third Sunday of February in the Oamaru Public Gardens. Whitestone had their twentieth anniversary last year, and Fleur enjoyed sharing the celebrations with them.

The Berry family, owners of Whitestone Cheese, enjoy an alfresco lunch at Fleurs Place.

02/

winter

For those curious to learn about the genesis of Fleurs Place, Fleur has compiled a scrapbook illustrating the early days of the restaurant. The boat shed-cum-apartment that originally stood on the site was pulled down, with only a single wall remaining as the basis for the new building. The timber for the beams and floors was salvaged from a dilapidated shed on Owen McCone's farm at Maheno, south of Oamaru – a shed that had originally stood on the wharf at Kakanui and had been shifted by two six-horse teams to a railway siding at Maheno.

Fleur tells an amusing story about the way in which she came by the old shed, after several trips to Maheno to negotiate a price. 'The farmer was a bit forgetful, and he couldn't always recognise that it was me, the same person coming back, and he began to think that the shed was very much sought after. But it was only me – and so one day I said to him, "I'll pay you $1000 more than that other lady's offered". He agreed, and so I pulled down the shed and brought all the timber back.' She also got the building's impressive limestone piles which now sit outside the restaurant.

The album tells the rest of the story: Fleur opened a 'caravan-kitchen' where she sold soup made from fish frames 'while construction continued in the background.' In November 2002 'service moved indoors' and Fleur's occasional outdoor catering

service segued into the restaurant as we know it today. Suggestions for a name included The Whale's Wake, in punning homage to the village's early European history. However, the restaurant acquired its present name as a result of the never-ending query, 'When's Fleur's place going to be finished?'

A humble 'shack'

It was never Fleur's intention to make a big splash in Moeraki. She wanted the restaurant to fit into the village, to be the kind of unpretentious building that would reflect its location on the site of the original nineteenth-century whaling station. 'People say it's hard to find. Good. I'm pleased it doesn't stick out! I'm pleased it doesn't have to have signs on it – it's just a simple building of the kind which would have been here in the old days.' With its recycled timbers and eclectic furnishings, the restaurant has a cobbled-together look and feel that is the polar opposite of flashy. 'A lot of American visitors say, "Oh, it's just a little tin shack." That's good!'

The smokehouse

Fleur takes great pride in showing visitors the smokehouse that sits outside the restaurant and is always full of fish

Inside the smokehouse.

heads, frames and wings – utilising the parts that other restaurants would have no occasion to use. Salmon frames are smoked after their fillets have been used fresh, and whole fish such as gurnard, moki, ling, rig and mako shark, flounder and mussels are also prepared here. Untreated manuka wood chips provide the fuel, and fennel stalks and bay leaves at times add to the heady aroma.

Fleur was keen to experiment with this way of preparing seafood after her arrival in Moeraki and a small portable smoker was put to good use in the catering caravan that preceded the restaurant on the wharf. As she herself admits, her early efforts represented a fairly steep learning curve. Fleur ruefully recalls the time that she proudly took an early batch of smoked cod heads to the local marae, 'to check if I was doing things right ... People were too polite to tell me that I'd left the gills in!'

Although Olivers in Clyde had a smoker built in the goldmining days, which she used to cure pork and rabbit meat, smoking food had never been part of her family's culinary tradition. 'In the small farming background that I came from, there was always plenty more the next day. We didn't have to preserve anything, really. The creek was there, the trout were there, the koura were there, the little fingerling eels were there and there was no real reason to preserve anything.' But Moeraki was different: 'Smoked seafood was intended to be a drawcard – a sign reading "Smoked Fish, Soup and Bread" was meant to lure people off the highway. The kaimoana platter was devised to give people a taste of different kinds of fish and it's now become a mainstay of the restaurant.'

The wines

During the 20 years she spent at Olivers, Fleur was well placed to observe the rise of the Central Otago wine industry. A small group of pioneer grape growers would meet regularly in the restaurant to discuss the joys and trials of their fledgling industry, and Fleur recalls with obvious pride that 'it was a wonderful day when I hung out a sign saying "food and wine of the region"'. She mentions names such as Verdun Burgess and Sue Edwards of Black Ridge, Alan Brady of Gibbston Valley in the Wakatipu Basin and Rolfe and Lois Mills of Rippon Winery near Wanaka – now all major players in a relatively small regional industry with an international reputation for quality and innovation.

Central Otago wines figure heavily on the wine list at Fleurs Place – Black Ridge, Dry Gully, Gibbston Valley, Rock 'n' Pillar, Thyme Hill, Two Paddocks, Carrick, Mt Maude, Mt Difficulty, Pisa Range ... 'But we've got a good red from the North Island and I think we've still got one Australian Cab Sav'. And Fleur is excited by the prospects of the Waitaki Valley, New Zealand's newest wine-growing region, which is already producing award-winning Pinot Noirs. Fleur feels that New Zealanders are more confident about asking for the wine they like, and that, today, people are not in the least pretentious about wine. Diners are adventurous and 'no one worries any more if they choose a good red to go with their fish dish'. She notes that, this last long hot summer (2007–2008), Rieslings and Gewurztraminers have been particularly popular, whereas the previous summer Pinot Gris was the wine most people asked for.

Head chef Simon Peacock.

Head chef

Head chef Simon Peacock takes pride in being a local boy made good. Raised in Alexandra, he was head boy at Dunstan High School and got his first job in the catering trade as a kitchenhand at the Millbrook Resort in Queenstown. After gaining professional qualifications in Christchurch, he worked for six years in the UK before returning to New Zealand in 2006 where he landed every young chef's dream job – personal chef for millionaire businessman Alan Gibbs at his estate in Kaukapakapa north of Auckland.

Growing up in Central Otago, Simon became aware of Fleur and her approach to food. As a schoolboy, he had explored her restaurant in Clyde and his sister had got married there. 'Olivers was part of the inspiration for me becoming a chef.' When he saw the advertisement for a head chef at Fleurs Place in early 2007, he felt he already knew the place.

Sure enough, Simon says that working here is 'Fantastic. Perfect.' He is in tune with Fleur's food philosophy, too, and his culinary style builds on that of illustrious predecessors such as French chef Gilbert Prevost, who followed Fleur to Moeraki from Olivers. In the UK Simon had worked in two small Michelin-star restaurants with a commitment to regional, locally sourced cuisine. So specialising in locally caught fish dishes is no problem – in fact, it fits right in with his own ambitions as a chef.

winter recipes

'Every month, we use around a tonne of mussels from the Hairy Mussel Company, and much gossip is exchanged as every spare pair of hands is put to the task of scraping them. Our European clients – including Rick Stein – simply cannot believe the quality, flavour and colour of our New Zealand green-lipped mussels.'

Smoked Marinated Mussels

ingredients

- 1 tsp fennel seeds
- 1 tsp peppercorns
- 1 tsp mustard seeds
- 3 star anise
- 2 lemons, sliced
- 2 red chillies, deseeded and sliced
- 1 handful coriander, chopped
- 3 bay leaves
- 1 inch fresh ginger, thinly sliced
- 50 g palm sugar
- 50 g brown sugar
- 100 ml soy sauce
- 50 ml sesame oil
- 200 ml olive oil
- 75 ml lemon juice
- 75 ml white wine vinegar
- 3 dozen green-lipped mussels

method

1 Toast the spices in a moderate oven for five minutes and grind down in a pestle and mortar.

2 Add this to the sliced lemons, chillies, coriander, bay leaves and ginger.

3 Crush the palm sugar and brown sugar and dissolve in the liquids.

4 Combine all ingredients (except mussels) and allow to infuse.

5 Steam mussels until just starting to open.

6 Remove meat from shells and toss in one teaspoon of olive oil. Smoke slowly in a wood smoker to manufacturer's instructions over untreated manuka woodchips.

7 While still warm, drop smoked mussels into marinade and enjoy.

'This dish was created at the Blues Bar in Clyde by a young chef called Brendan and perfected with the Pernod by Fiona in Moeraki.'

serves four

Aotearoa Scallops with Pernod

method

1 Ensure scallops are clean. Remove sinews and pat dry.
2 In a large frying-pan, soften the onion and garlic in the butter.
3 Add bacon lardons and mushrooms and cook for 2–3 minutes.
4 Transfer vegetables and bacon to a separate bowl.
5 Heat the pan again and add scallops to cover base of frying-pan. Cook 2 minutes on one side, turn and add vegetables and bacon back in.
6 Deglaze pan by adding Pernod and allow to flame.
7 Add the cream, cook for a further 2 minutes and then serve.

ingredients

24 Nelson scallops
1 onion, finely chopped
1 clove garlic, crushed
50 g butter
200 g belly bacon from Fleur's smokehouse, cut into lardons
6 button mushrooms, sliced
100 ml Pernod
200 ml cream

Fleurs Place

Place
food

'The rabbit, venison and pickled walnut pie is something I did in Clyde. People still associate me with that dish and ask if I will do it for them. People ring me up for the recipe, especially venison farmers. I used to do my own pickled walnuts, but in Clyde I formed a special arrangement with Ian Mair of Stonehouse Products – I'd give him the walnuts and he'd do the work! Stonehouse do a blackberry pickle that goes really nicely with it as well.'

serves eight

Rabbit, Venison & Pickled Walnut Pie

ingredients

For the stock

- rabbit bones
- 1 onion, 1 carrot, 1 stick celery and 4 cloves garlic, chopped
- 1 cup red wine

For the filling

- 1 large onion, chopped
- 2 cloves garlic, crushed
- 3 slices smoked pork belly (or streaky bacon)
- olive oil
- 750 g diced rabbit meat (saving the bones for the stock)
- 750 g diced venison
- 2 tbsp flour
- 1 tbsp seeded mustard
- 1 tbsp tomato purée
- 1 tbsp fresh thyme, chopped
- 2 tbsp parsley, chopped
- 1 tbsp Worcestershire sauce
- 80 g mushrooms, washed and halved
- 12 pickled walnuts
- salt and pepper

For the case

- 250 g puff or short crust pastry
- 1 egg yolk or milk

method

1 Make stock by roasting bones and vegetables in the oven until they begin to caramelise. This should take about 30 minutes.
2 Transfer to a pot with the red wine and just cover with water. Simmer for 1½ hours.
3 Strain the liquid off, discard the solids and reduce to one cup by hard boiling.
4 Season to taste.
5 Make the filling by sautéing the onion, garlic and pork belly in a little olive oil.
6 Add rabbit and venison and brown.
7 Stir in the flour until it disappears, then add the stock, mustard, tomato purée, herbs and Worcestershire sauce. Cover and simmer gently for 45 minutes.
8 Add mushrooms and pickled walnuts, and season with salt and freshly ground pepper.
9 What you bake the pie in is now up to you. Fleur suggests large muffin tins, but you could also use ramekins or small pudding bowls - or throw the whole lot into a large pie dish. Line your chosen container with rolled-out pastry, fill, cover, brush with egg yolk or milk and crimp the edges together. Make a hole in the top of the pie with a skewer and decorate with pastry leaves and pastry walnuts.
10 Heat the oven to 220 °C and bake the pie for 30 minutes.

Fleur serves these pies with quince paste and seasonal vegetables.

'This is a convenient way of producing a delicious dish from the ham hocks which we cure and smoke ourselves.' (Head chef Simon Peacock)

makes one standard terrine dish

Ham Hock Terrine

method

1 If the ham hocks are known to be salty, soak in cold water in the refrigerator overnight and discard the water.

2 Place ham hocks, vegetables, spices and herbs in a large pot and cover with fresh cold water.

3 Boil gently for around two hours or until the meat appears to be falling off the bone.

4 Transfer the meat to a tray to cool; strain the liquid, reserving the liquor and discarding the vegetables.

5 Boil the ham liquid and reduce down to around 250 ml; dissolve the gelatine in this.

6 Pick through the ham hocks removing all bones, fat and gristle. Take care not to break the meat up too much.

7 Mix through the mustard and parsley and a third of the reduced liquor.

8 Press into a terrine dish or loaf tin that has been lined with cling film. Pour over remaining liquid and refrigerate overnight.

Serve slices with homemade pickled onions, gherkins and a fiery hot mustard as a ploughman's lunch.

ingredients

4 smoked ham hocks
2 sticks celery
1 carrot
1 onion
4 cloves garlic
peppercorns, bay leaves and thyme stalks
1 leaf gelatine
2 tbsp wholegrain mustard
1 large handful parsley, chopped

'This is the answer for the hurried traveller or the bloke who can't be bothered reading the menu and wants "just a bit of blue cod".'

Blue Cod on Rewena Bread with Homemade Brown Sauce

ingredients

- fresh blue cod fillets
- seasoned flour for dusting
- vegetable oil and butter for frying
- your favourite bread, e.g. rewena or sourdough

Brown sauce

makes 3 litres

- 4 kg tomatoes, chopped
- 1 litre malt vinegar
- 1 litre cider vinegar
- 1 tsp black peppercorns
- 2 kg brown sugar
- 200 g sultanas
- 2 kg cooking apples, peeled and chopped
- 8 dried chillies
- 1 tsp cayenne pepper
- 3 bay leaves
- 1 kg chopped onions
- 6 tsp mustard powder
- 8 whole star anise
- 500 g prunes, pitted

method

1 Dust the blue cod fillets with the flour and place into a warmed, non-stick pan with the vegetable oil.

2 Dot small knobs of butter around the fish and fry gently in the golden bubbling butter. Do not allow the butter to burn.

3 Gently turn the fish after a couple of minutes or when a soft golden colour appears on the underside. Cook for a couple of minutes more, then take from the heat and allow the heat from the pan to finish cooking the fish while you prepare the rest of the sandwich.

4 Sandwich the blue cod in the bread. Depending on what part of the world you're from, serve with homemade tomato or brown sauce, a little bit of salad and some lemon wedges.

Brown sauce

1 In a large preserving pan, place all the ingredients and bring to the boil while stirring.

2 Simmer gently for 1–1½ hours until thick.

3 Pass through a moulis and bottle in sterilised jars.

'I am fortunate indeed to have known the three best boil-up cooks in the world, Mary Whitau, Julian McKay and Paaka Westrup. Mary would have to be the "best of the best" because Julian lives in Southland, Paaka is buried in Gisborne and Mary is alive and well in Moeraki. Thank you, Mary, for all those phone calls – "do you want some boil-up later?".'

serves six to eight

Boil-up for Staff with Pork Bones, Cabbage & Kumara

ingredients

- 2 kg pork bones from the rib
- 6 litres water
- salt
- 4 carrots, peeled and chopped
- 6 kumara, peeled
- 6 potatoes, preferably waxy
- 1 head cabbage
- 2 handfuls watercress

method

1 Place the pork bones in a large pot with a lid and cover with the water.
2 Add a heaped teaspoon of salt for the bones and one for every kind of vegetable you will be adding later. Bring to the boil, then turn the heat down and allow to simmer for around an hour.
3 Check the water levels and add more if required. Add the root vegetables and continue to cook until just tender.
4 Cut the cabbage into quarters and place over the top of the boil-up, replace the lid and steam for 10–15 minutes.
5 Drop handfuls of fresh watercress in just before serving.

This is best served the next day with plenty of bread and butter.

'This dish is especially fun – fun watching the customers' faces when you put the bowl in front of them, fun gathering the watercress, fun sourcing the Maori potatoes . . .'

serves four

Shellfish Hotpot

ingredients

- aromatics such as garlic, lemongrass, lime leaves, bay, ginger
- 500 ml fish stock
- 200 ml white wine
- 1 good pinch saffron
- 8 fillets fresh fish
- 24 mussels, washed and debearded
- 24 littleneck clams, washed
- 24 queen shell scallops
- 6 spring onions, chopped
- 1 handful chopped parsley
- 16 gourmet or Maori potatoes, pre-boiled
- washed spinach or watercress

method

1 Infuse the aromatics in the fish stock by slowly bringing to just below boiling and allow to sit.

2 In a separate pan place the wine and saffron and bring to the boil. Reduce the wine by about a half, allowing the colour from the saffron to come out.

3 Strain the fish stock through a fine sieve and add to the wine. Place the fish and shellfish in the broth, cover with a lid and simmer gently for 5 minutes. Lift the lid, add the remaining ingredients, replace the lid and simmer for a further 2 or 3 minutes or until the fish is cooked and the shellfish open.

4 Divide equally into 4 bowls and serve.

Catch of the Day
Greek Salad w Whitestone Feta
Mussel Linguine w Basil Pesto
Shellfish Hotpot w saffron broth, fresh fish & Maori Potatoes

RECKITTS BAG BLUE
the cookbook tour

'Rice and sago pudding sells well at the restaurant all year round – but especially when the coal range is burning inside and the sea breeze is biting out. The promise of mother's cooking causes a flurry of nostalgic excitement whenever this dish is posted on the dessert board. One older gentleman ordered the sago pudding purely to see what the kitchen could produce from something that had traditionally cost one shilling and sixpence a pound. (Needless to say, he was suitably impressed.)'

serves ten

Rice Pudding with Mulled Tamarillos

ingredients

- 450 g pudding rice (short grain)
- 1 litre milk
- 160 g caster sugar
- 100 ml cream
- 2 vanilla pods, split lengthways and the seeds scraped out
- 400 g sweetened condensed milk
- 100 g butter

Tamarillos poached in mulled wine

- 500 ml fruity red wine
- 200 g brown sugar
- 2 cinnamon sticks
- 3 whole cloves
- 3 whole star anise
- 1 orange, zest only
- 1 lemon, zest only
- 10 firm but ripe tamarillos

method

1 Wash rice in cold water and drain well.

2 In a heavy-bottomed pot combine rice, milk, caster sugar, cream and vanilla seeds (and pods) and bring to simmer on a low heat. Stir occasionally to avoid the mixture sticking and simmer until the rice is tender and liquid absorbed (add a little more milk if too thick).

3 Finish by stirring through the condensed milk and butter. Remove pods before serving.

Variation

To make a sago pudding, replace the rice with 270 g sago.

Tamarillos poached in mulled wine

1 In a saucepan large enough to hold all the tamarillos, place all ingredients except tamarillos and carefully bring to the boil.

2 Take off the heat and allow to infuse.

3 Nick the undersides of the tamarillos lightly with a paring knife. In a pan of boiling water, drop in the tamarillos for 30 seconds and then transfer to iced water. This will allow you to peel off the tough skins, leaving the fruit intact.

4 Submerge peeled tamarillos in the mulled wine and return to a gentle simmer until just tender and the spices have permeated the fruit.

'People get excited about classic puddings and desserts like this because they evoke such rich childhood memories.' (Head chef Simon Peacock)

serves eight

Treacle Tart

ingredients

180 g brown breadcrumbs, toasted
75 g butter
1 lemon, juiced
900 g golden syrup
2 lemons, zested
75 ml cream
1 tsp salt
3 eggs
1 x 25-cm flan dish pastry case, blind baked

method

1 Preheat oven to 170 °C.
2 Toast breadcrumbs until pale and golden.
3 Heat butter in a saucepan until it begins to brown.
4 When butter begins to smell nutty, add lemon juice.
5 Add golden syrup and warm gently.
6 Add the breadcrumbs to the syrup and mix along with the lemon zest, cream, salt and lastly the eggs.
7 Pour into pre-prepared pastry case and cook for 25–30 minutes or until it seems firm in the centre of the tart.

Allow to cool and serve with crème anglaise and whipped cream.

'An Irish aunt who would have been 80 when I was 25 or so gave me this easy recipe handed down from her family. It never fails – just sometimes the pudding is better than others. It can be frozen, eaten cold and sliced like a loaf, fried in a pan for breakfast, and made in any size and variety of bowls – with or without jam in the bottom. It can be delivered to all and sundry at any time of the year – but you are more likely to be plied with sherry, gin or double Baileys during the festive season.'

Mid-Winter Christmas Puddings

ingredients

- 450 g butter
- 2 litres milk
- ½ tin golden syrup
- 2 cups caster sugar
- 2½ kg dried fruit including sultanas, mixed peel, dried Central Otago fruit, etc.
- 3 tsp baking soda
- 4 cups plain flour
- 1 tsp baking powder

Brandy butter

- 200 g unsalted butter
- 1 cup icing sugar
- 4–8 tbsp brandy

Rum sauce

- 2 cups milk
- ½ cup cream
- 150 g caster sugar
- 2 tbsp cornflour
- ½ cup rum

method

1. In a heavy-bottomed pot bring butter, milk, golden syrup and caster sugar up to the boil.
2. Add dried fruit and simmer gently for 10 minutes. Remove from heat and leave overnight or up to three days.
3. Return to heat and bring back to the boil (it may appear split, but do not panic).
4. Add baking soda and allow to bubble.
5. Fold through flour and baking powder.
6. Transfer to a well-greased pudding bowl and steam for 1½–2 hours or until a skewer comes out clean.

Hints

Start with a large pot and, if your mixture remains too sticky, add more flour and baking powder. You will need a strong arm and a sturdy wooden spoon.

Brandy butter

Cream the butter and sugar until pale and creamy. Add the brandy drop by drop and keep just below room temperature.

Rum sauce

1. In a saucepan bring the milk and cream to a gentle simmer.
2. Add the sugar and stir to dissolve.
3. Mix the cornflour and rum together to form a thin paste.
4. Add the rum mixture to the milk and cream whilst stirring and cook out for 2–3 minutes until smooth and glossy.

'It's always good to have something on the menu for chocolate-lovers, and this certainly hits the spot.' (Head chef Simon Peacock)

serves eight

Chocolate Marquise

ingredients

215 g chocolate
12 egg yolks
2 shots espresso
270 g icing sugar
170 g cocoa
120 g honey
360 g butter, soft, at room temperature
280 ml whipped cream

method

1 Melt chocolate in a double boiler, remove from heat and drop in egg yolks, beat until smooth and satiny.

2 Mix together espresso, sugar, cocoa and honey to create a paste. Beat until smooth, adding a little warm water until workable.

3 Cream butter in a large mixing bowl, add cocoa paste and beat until smooth. Fold in chocolate mixture and (lastly) whipped cream.

4 Pour into a greased terrine dish (or loaf pan) lined with cling film. Chill 2 hours before serving.

Dessert chef Heather Wollaston holds a bountiful bowl of blackcurrants from the Hampden garden of Bob Williams and Lesley Hale.

'Keeping the "circle" of scones compact ensures they rise. Place on the table, covered with a linen tea towel.'

serves eight

Girdle Scones with Homemade Blackcurrant Jam

method

1 Sift flour, baking powder and salt together in a bowl.

2 Rub in the butter until the mixture resembles fine breadcrumbs.

3 Add sufficient milk to make a fairly soft dough.

4 On a lightly floured board, roll out to 1-cm thickness. Shape into a round and cut into 8 wedges.

5 Cook on a hot greased girdle on top of the stove for about 5 minutes or until freckled brown. Turn over, reforming the round and cook until freckled on the other side.

6 Serve with generous quantities of our blackcurrant jam.

ingredients

1 cup standard plain flour
2 tsp baking powder
pinch of salt
1 tbsp butter
½ cup milk, approximately
blackcurrant jam (see next recipe)

'Makes a great topping for your rice or sago puddings or your porridge. Also put a spoonful of jam in a cup and pour in boiling water for a delicious drink.'

makes about 4 x 350-ml jars

Blackcurrant Jam

ingredients

1 kg blackcurrants

2 cups water

6 cups sugar

method

1 Remove stalks from blackcurrants.

2 Place in a preserving pan with the water and boil gently until the fruit is soft.

3 Add the sugar and stir until dissolved. Bring to the boil and boil rapidly for 15 minutes or until setting point is reached.

4 Pour into sterilised jars.

spring

03/

Alison McTavish

Alison McTavish has been supplying Fleurs Place with a daily bundle of premier herbs and vegetables from her rambling Moeraki garden since 2005. She picks herbs like Italian parsley, mint, coriander, bronze fennel, sweet basil and salad burnet from a tiny sheltered bed beside the house. Alison gathers an abundance of mainly green vegetables – Chinese brassica, Romanescu and purple-sprouting broccoli, lettuces, cauliflowers (Violet Sicilian), kohlrabi, yams (anu), Florence fennel, rhubarb, cavalo nero (an Italian brassica with tiny leaves used in salads) and miner's purslane, to name but a few – from beds laid out on a sunny north-facing slope.

A former teacher at Waitaki Girls' High School, Alison has started up produce markets in nearby Hampden, gives demonstration classes in food preservation in the town library and talks enthusiastically of a 'Hampden hamper' scheme that would bring fresh country produce into urban kitchens. One gets the impression that Alison's career as a gardener and advocate of fresh, locally-grown food has only just begun. There is plenty of room on the property for expansion and her husband Dugald has begun laying out lengths of old carpet as the basis for permaculture beds.

The are a number of strands to the relationship between Alison and Fleur, going back to the old catering caravan days. Alison's daughter, Jinty, was an early worker in the restaurant and her zeal for recycling led Fleur to dub her 'my little conscience'. And Jinty's brother, Tom, worked on the fishing boats as a university student.

As a grower, Alison's relationship with Fleur has developed gradually, in response to the restaurant's needs and the gardener's capacity to supply them. Fleur is a little envious of her green-fingered neighbour: 'She's doing what I want to do – growing all these beautiful things and bringing them here, whereas I had expected the restaurant to be small enough to have its own kitchen garden. She grows what she can manage – we're not demanding of her – we'll take whatever she has in at the time. She doesn't overpick, and if the sun's too strong or the weather's too wet she doesn't pick at all. So we're at her mercy.' And the mercy of the seasons.

For Alison McTavish, Fleur is a latter-day exponent of the ancient Ngai Tahu tradition of mahinga kai or the gathering of food from local resources, 'the food of the place'. Following the harvest of the all-surrounding sea, complementary tastes are sought out from the land. Just as eel and watercress co-exist in life, so their flavours match and enhance each other. As Alison sees it, Fleur seeks to create a culinary economy that is unique to this place and its history. 'Fleur has a mind-map tucked away in her head of all the wild apple trees, the patches of cress, where the wild fennel will sprout in the spring, the potential abundance of the land. Why does the Moeraki potato go with muttonbird, and why do they look so good with New Zealand spinach? The dish captures a flavour which isn't just the flavour of the taste buds. If we wish to savour our traditions, the muttonbird makes the mind fly to the southern islands and hardy Maori hunters, the New Zealand spinach to Captain Cook looking for vitamin-filled antidotes

Grower Alison McTavish in the potato patch of her Moeraki garden.

to scurvy, and the Moeraki potato is a window on the dinner plates of our whaling ancestors.'

The Moeraki potato

Known to the early whalers as 'Old Red', the Moeraki potato once grew wild on empty sections on the peninsula, but is now carefully cultivated by Alison along with several other varieties of Maori potato. Variable in size and knobbly, the Moeraki potato is purple on the outside and white flecked with purple within. Possibly the descendant of potatoes planted by Captain Cook in Queen Charlotte Sound in 1773, it was nurtured by Maori gardeners and in the 1830s and '40s brought south to whaling stations like Moeraki. Fleur uses this heritage spud in her muttonbird confit, which is also served with New Zealand spinach supplied by Alison.

Chris Larcombe and Viviene Scott

After three seasons at the Otago Farmers' Market, Chris Larcombe and Viviene Scott of Kakanui Produce are old hands. Each Saturday morning, they leave their North Otago base at 5.30 a.m. and are set up in their regular possie in the market by 7 a.m. when the first punters arrive.

Opposite: Alison McTavish holds Maori potatoes freshly dug from her Moeraki garden. **Above:** North Otago growers Chris Larcombe and Viviene Scott at their stall in the Otago Farmers' Market at the Dunedin Railway Station.

Their stall has a strong focus on tomatoes – a speciality of the rich soils of Kakanui, a traditional market-gardening district just south of Oamaru – and the dozen or so varieties on offer comprise low-acid, cherry, cocktail and table types. Viviene propagates their tomatoes from seed and skilfully grafts the plants herself. But their stall is also bursting with a profusion of vegetables including cucumbers, capsicum, chillies, brassicas, courgettes and potatoes (jersey bennies and red kings).

Their first contact with Fleur was informality itself – they simply dropped in at Moeraki on their way home from the market one Saturday afternoon and showed her what they had left. Now head chef Simon Peacock places detailed orders with them every week – today they have prepared several trays of mixed herbs and salad mixes which, planted out in soil-filled pottles, will last a week or so of regular picking with a little watering. Viviene confides that chef is particularly partial to their basil, bull's horn capsicum and, of course, their tomatoes.

According to Viviene, the staff at Fleurs Place have a character all their own. 'Here's the vege lady', is the cheery call that greets her every weekend. There's always a good laugh to be had inside or out down at the old wharf at Moeraki.

Colin Dennison

Colin Dennison of Evansdale Cheese has been a fixture of the Otago Farmers' Market since its inception in 2003 and from his stall he beckons the unwary punter with offers of cheesey delights – a theatrical role for which his long career as a schoolteacher has well fitted him. Now a full-time artisan cheesemaker, he takes an obvious pride in his boast that he makes cheese almost every day of the year.

Colin set up the business at Evansdale just north of Dunedin 30 years ago, and relocated to the former Cherry Farm hospital site in 1998. The company makes 50 tons of cheese a year, and sells its products to farmers' markets and restaurants and delis, and direct to individual customers. Colin began exporting to Australia in 2007 and is developing an on-site tourist centre to cope with the growing interest in the Evansdale product. Although scornful of supermarkets ('who wants to buy broccoli from China?'), he can't resist telling the story of the supermarket owner who set up a farmers' market in his car park.

Fleur makes regular purchasing trips to the factory to select the salty, milky curd cheese that is the basis for her curd tart with dried blueberries and is always made the same day as it's sold (it undergoes a change in structure after a day or two). While there, she may well pick out other cheeses with names like Komene Kass, Laurel's Farmhouse brie and Tania, and perhaps a wedge or two of Marilyn's Blue.

Roger Belton

Surprisingly, Kiwis have been slow to cotton on to the shellfish cornucopia on their back doorstep. While Roger Belton, managing director of Southern Clams Limited, arranges regular export consignments of littleneck clams and vongoli (the smallest grade of clam, also known as pasta) to Boston and Rome, the domestic market makes up only 10–15 per cent of total orders. One still hears clams dismissed sniffily as 'cockles'

Evansdale Cheese proprietor Colin Dennison prepares samples of his wares at the Otago Farmers' Market.

CHEESE

Roger Belton of Southern Clams with a sack of freshly dredged littleneck clams from Blueskin Bay.

in some quarters. But local tastes are changing, as anyone who has savoured Southern Clams' succulent molluscs in Fleur's seafood chowder will attest.

Based in Dunedin, Southern Clams are well placed to take advantage of the bivalve bounty of the South. According to Roger, Otago has the biggest and best littleneck clam resource in the country – in the clear waters of Blueskin Bay near Waitati and Papanui Inlet on Otago Peninsula, where they are harvested by hand-raking (or 'body dredge'), they grow larger than anywhere else. And the queen scallops that the company also harvests in season are found only on the edge of the continental shelf that lies off the Otago and Southland coasts.

Roger first met Fleur in the early 1980s when he was researching the viability of a clam fishery, and was impressed by her immediate enthusiasm and keenness to work with local seafood products, even as far from the coast as Central Otago. In those days the firm transported shellfish to Clyde by bus, protected from blazing summer temperatures only by polystyrene packaging. Nowadays, Roger's clams are chilled (never frozen) to keep them in a state of suspended animation and Fleur's regular consignment arrives on her doorstep live and fresh – just the way she wants them.

Gavin Te Maiharoa

Gavin Te Maiharoa's boat, the *Matai*, is now one of only four working the Moeraki fishery – a far cry from the fleet of 40-odd boats that worked these grounds in the heyday of the industry around 1900, and even the 25 or so boats that were still active in the late 1990s. So important was sea-fishing to the village that a fish-freezing factory was established here in 1895. Today, blue cod and hapuku (groper) are important species caught here, and crayfish or rock lobster are still taken in good numbers.

Gavin goes fishing most days in suitable weather and, as Moeraki is an inshore fishery, ventures no further out than 30 km or so. Using set nets

58

and trawling gear, he and his crewmate had brought in a haul of school shark, moki and elephant fish on the flawless January evening I chatted with them as they soaked up the evening sun over a glass of beer outside Fleurs Place. There was no blue cod that day because, as Gavin explained, there is little return from the baited pots used to catch them over the summer months when their natural food is abundant.

Gavin has been fishing for Fleur for four years, using her personal quota, and has been working out of Moeraki for more years than he can remember. He also supplies fish for Motueka-based Talley's Fisheries and after each trip hauls blue plastic bins full of gutted fish into a container on the wharf. As one of the last practitioners of a dying local tradition, he acknowledges that – with government bureaucracy, rising diesel prices and competition from big foreign companies – commercial fishing is not an easy life and he is uncertain what the future may hold. Still, as Fleur wryly observes, Gavin often takes his young daughter out fishing with him on the *Matai*.

Moeraki fisherman Gavin Te Maiharoa on his boat at the Moeraki fisherman's wharf. **Opposite:** *Matai* returns to its home port after a day's fishing at sea.

Susan Randell of Mean Greens drops off an order at Fleurs Place. **Opposite:** Watercress freshly picked from a garden behind the Moeraki marae (see recipe on page 120).

'This is a fish restaurant,' says head chef Simon Peacock, 'and if it wasn't for Gavin going out every day and catching us fish, we wouldn't be in business.' He proceeds to rattle off a list of the fish caught locally: blue cod, moki, monkfish, groper, trumpeter, skate, gurnard, tarakihi, sole, flounder, brill. Sea perch and red cod are taken mainly for smoking, as well as rig and mako shark, which is treated like tuna for its succulent steaks.

Susan Randell

Most Thursday mornings, Susan Randell swings past Fleurs Place with a swag of edible greenery. Each day she picks to order from a wide selection of 'salady things' – fancy lettuce, watercress, rocket, mesclun, mizuna – grown in a 1000 m^2 hydroponic greenhouse in Oamaru. Susan started her business, Mean Greens, in 2000 and the feedback was so positive that she decided to market her salad greens direct to chefs who value a reliable supply of top-quality, fresh produce. Now she and co-worker Katrina Moffatt supply many restaurants and four wholesalers in Timaru, Dunedin and Central Otago as well as Oamaru. Susan says that she's never had to advertise.

Mean Greens is by no means a small operation. There are 18,000 lettuces and 20,000 seedlings in the greenhouse at any one time, and a ton of greenery is produced every month. Despite this, the small team handles all the firm's packaging and freight needs.

'I love Moeraki – it's unspoilt,' says Susan. 'And I love coming down to Fleurs Place. The building has fantastic character and the food is marvellous.' Like all Fleur's suppliers, she is very much in tune with her client's needs. 'Our hallmarks are fresh, locally grown, good quality – Fleur emphasises that, too. Fleur is the type of customer we seek.' And vice versa.

spring recipes

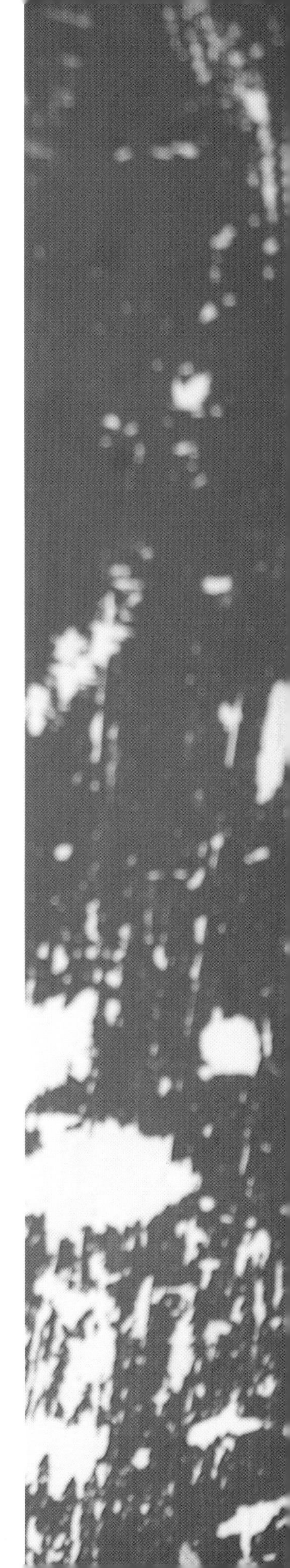

'To be able to gather watercress from a running stream on a beautiful morning on your way to work gives a feeling of freedom that few city chefs can experience.'

serves four

Watercress Soup with Soft Poached Egg

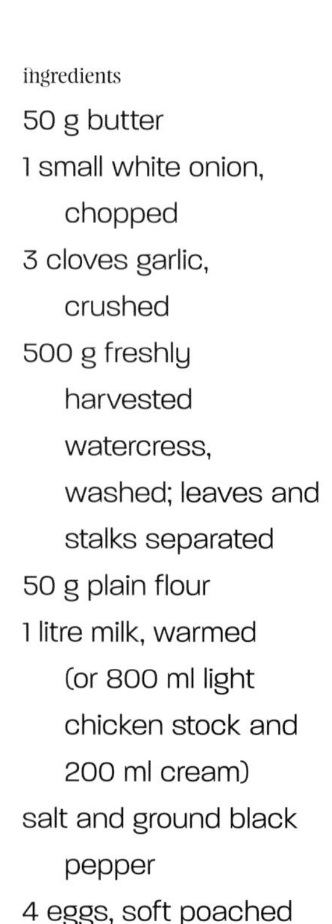

ingredients

50 g butter
1 small white onion, chopped
3 cloves garlic, crushed
500 g freshly harvested watercress, washed; leaves and stalks separated
50 g plain flour
1 litre milk, warmed (or 800 ml light chicken stock and 200 ml cream)
salt and ground black pepper
4 eggs, soft poached

method

1 In a heavy-bottomed pot, melt butter gently and sweat onion, garlic and watercress stalks until tender but not coloured.

2 Add flour and cook for a further two minutes.

3 Add a cup of the warmed milk and stir until thickened and lumps of flour are removed.

4 Keep adding milk slowly and allow to gently come to the boil.

5 Add the leaves of the watercress and purée immediately until smooth and a vibrant green colour is achieved.

6 Season with salt and pepper and serve hot with a soft poached egg and a drizzle of good olive oil.

'This recipe evolved from Shona Sinclair's chowder that we sold from the caravan "before the restaurant". It was originally served in a pan on an old-fashioned breadboard – and I know lots of our soup-lovers would love to see it served this way again.'

serves eight to ten

Fleur's Seafood Chowder

ingredients

200 g butter
1 onion, diced
2 carrots, diced
2 sticks celery, diced
200 g flour
100 ml white wine
150 g tomato paste
2 litres fish stock, warmed
1 tsp fennel seeds, ground
1 tsp smoked paprika
2 bay leaves
1 tsp fresh thyme or sprigs of wild Cental Otago thyme, chopped
500 g fish, diced
20 mussels, picked and washed
30 littleneck clams, washed
20 queen scallops, washed

method

1 In a large heavy-bottomed pot melt the butter and add the diced vegetables. Sweat for a couple of minutes but do not allow to colour.

2 Add the flour and cook for a further 2 minutes or until it has a sandy texture.

3 Slowly pour in the wine and tomato paste and bring together as it thickens to remove all the lumps.

4 Add the warmed fish stock slowly, stirring continuously, and drop in the herbs and spices.

5 Allow all this to come to the boil, taking care not to catch the bottom of the pan.

6 Add all the fish and shellfish and simmer until the shells begin to open (only 2 or 3 minutes) and the fish is cooked through.

Head chef Simon says: 'This simple salad lives or dies on the quality of each individual ingredient. We offer this dish on our menu whenever there is a glut of tomatoes from our organic grower up the road in Hampden.'

serves two to three

Greek Salad

ingredients

- 3 or 4 ground-grown, height of season, sun-ripened tomatoes
- ½ cucumber
- ⅓ red onion
- 1 good handful of black kalamata olives
- 200 g feta (we use the organic Fuchsia Creek cows' milk feta from Whitestone Cheese)
- fresh oregano, chopped
- salt and pepper
- good olive oil and red wine vinegar

method

1 Dice all the ingredients into equal-sized chunks.

2 Mix gently and dress at the last minute with the olive oil and vinegar.

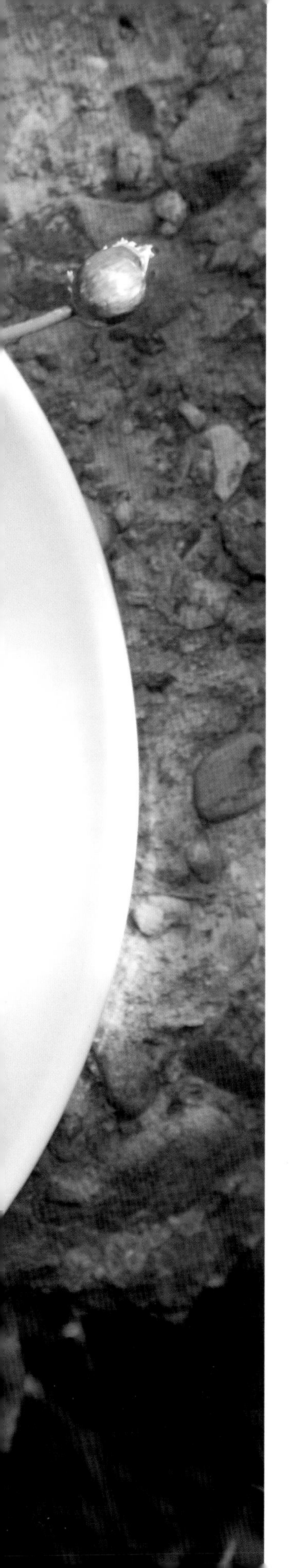

'For a truly local flavour, nothing beats the Moeraki platter as a dish to be enjoyed out on the balcony on a still, sunny day with a glass of Central Otago wine.' (Head chef Simon Peacock)

Moeraki Platter

The platter is made up of whatever ingredients are to hand. The selection here includes Whitestone brie, homemade pâté, pickled onions, gherkins, piccalilli, radishes, pickled red cabbage, boiled egg, roast Mediterranean vegetables and smoked flounder.

makes 8 x 350-ml jars

Piccalilli

Piccalilli

ingredients

- 3 kg chopped, mixed vegetables (including cauliflower, carrot, onion, peppers and cucumber)
- 1/2 cup salt
- 1 litre spiced vinegar
- 350 g brown sugar
- 2 tbsp dry mustard powder
- 1 tbsp turmeric
- 3 tbsp plain flour

method

1 Place the vegetables in a plastic or non-reacting stainless steel container and cover with salt. Leave overnight.
2 Place the remaining ingredients in a large heavy-bottomed pot and slowly bring to the boil. Simmer gently for three to five minutes until smooth, thick and glossy.
3 Wash and drain the vegetables, add to the spiced liquid and gently allow to come back to the boil. Pack into sterilised jars.

'We always keep an eye out for the time Rod Phillips' huge sign – ASPARAGUS – goes up outside his place between Moeraki and Palmerston. We get banana boxes-full delivered daily while the season lasts. Years ago in my Dunstan House days, my favourite place to gather asparagus was the Clyde Cemetery – I remember that the Naylor plot produced especially rich pickings.'

serves two

Asparagus with Hollandaise Sauce

ingredients

1 bunch new season's asparagus, woody ends trimmed
salt

Hollandaise

2 tbsp white wine vinegar
2 tbsp water
1 tsp white peppercorns, crushed
4 egg yolks
250 g unsalted butter, clarified
pinch cayenne pepper
2 lemons, juiced

method

1 Place vinegar, water and peppercorns in a small, heavy-based pan and bring to the boil. Reduce gently until 2–2½ tbsp remain.

2 Cool then strain into a heatproof, round-bottomed mixing bowl. Add egg yolks and whisk together.

3 Set the bowl over a pan of simmering water, but do not allow the bowl to touch the water. Whisk for 5–6 minutes or until it thickens, is pale and smooth and holds a ribbon when the whisk is lifted.

4 Set the bowl on a slip-proof mat. Slowly pour in the clarified butter in a thin stream while whisking, until thick and glossy.

5 Add the cayenne and lemon juice and season with salt and pepper. Serve at once or keep warm until you are ready.

'Mick's hens seem to know when the whitebait season has arrived and put in a supreme effort – although one year he had to buy more hens.'

serves one

Whitebait Omelette with Mick's Free-range Eggs

ingredients

- 2 of Mick's fresh free-range hens' eggs (or you could try duck eggs)
- 200 g new season's West Coast whitebait
- splash of cream
- vegetable oil
- 1 lemon and plenty of ground black pepper to serve

method

1 Heat a non-stick omelette pan on the element.
2 Crack the eggs in a bowl and whisk in the whitebait and cream with a fork.
3 Add the oil to the pan and allow it to begin to smoke. Add the egg mixture and work with the fork until it is two-thirds cooked, taking care not to colour it too much on the bottom.
4 Finish under a hot grill or in the oven until the omelette begins to rise or puff up. Do not overcook - leave it still slightly creamy in the centre.

Serve squeezed with lemon and dusted in pepper, with a slice of buttered bread on the side.

'Lamb dishes always do very well at the restaurant and I often find myself guessing who at the table will order the lamb.'

serves four

Irish Lamb Stew with Seaweed Dumplings & Glazed Carrots

method

1 Place diced lamb, onions, leeks, celery and garlic into a heavy-bottomed casserole dish.

2 Cover completely with lamb or chicken stock and gently bring to a rolling boil.

3 Cover with casserole lid and simmer gently for 1–1½ hours until lamb is very tender.

4 Drain the meat and vegetables in a colander, reserving the liquid, and keep meat warm by covering in aluminium foil.

5 Add potatoes and rosemary to the liquid and return to the boil. (Water can be added if too much evaporation has occurred.)

6 Cook until the potatoes are tender, purée the liquid until a smooth, sauce-like consistency occurs.

7 Season to taste and add warm lamb and vegetables back and warm through to serve.

8 Add chopped parsley just as you're serving.

Dumplings

1 Rub suet through the flour and baking powder until it resembles breadcrumbs.

2 Bring together with the seaweed, seasoning and enough milk to bind.

3 Roll into small balls – they will swell – and set on a floured board.

4 Poach off in boiling lamb stock for 3–4 minutes after they float to the top.

Carrots

1 Boil scrubbed and cleaned carrots in salted water until just tender.

2 Strain and reserve 2–3 tbsp water still in the saucepan with the carrots.

3 Add sugar and butter and move over a moderate heat until the liquid evaporates and the carrots are shiny and glazed.

Serve a hearty portion of the stew in deep bowls. Dot around with 3–4 dumplings (these can be prepared beforehand and warmed under a grill till ready) and garnish with glazed carrots.

ingredients

Stew

- 1 kg diced lean lamb
- 3 onions, peeled and chopped
- 2 leeks, diced
- 3 sticks celery, chopped
- 4 cloves garlic
- 3 litres lamb or chicken stock
- 6 large potatoes, peeled and chopped
- sprigs of rosemary
- chopped parsley

Dumplings

- 2 tbsp suet
- 2 cups plain flour
- 3 tsp baking powder
- 3 tbsp dried karengo (seaweed) flakes
- 1 tsp salt
- 1 cup milk

Carrots

- baby carrots
- salt
- 2 tsp sugar
- 1 tbsp butter

58

The *Matai* heads out of Moeraki for a day's fishing at sea.

> 'Carrying any whole baked fish into the dining area is always a thrill – and often gives rise to "food envy". Heads turn as people wonder if they should have ordered it.'

ingredients

- 4 small trumpeter, scaled and gutted and fins clipped (or a larger one for the table)
- 4 lemons, sliced
- a selection of freshly picked herbs including bay, parsley, lemon thyme, etc.
- olive oil
- salt and pepper
- 200 g butter
- 2 lemons, juiced
- 3 tbsp toasted almonds, slivered
- 3 tbsp capers
- 2 tbsp parsley, chopped

Caper and lime butter sauce

- 200 ml white wine
- 75 ml lime juice
- 200 ml cream
- 200 g cold butter, diced
- 2 tbsp capers

serves four

Whole Roast Trumpeter with Caper & Lime Butter Sauce

method

1 Preheat the oven to 190 °C.
2 Slash the trumpeter on both sides towards the head to ensure it cooks evenly. Stuff the cavity with lemon slices and the fresh herbs, drizzle with olive oil, season with salt and pepper and place on a baking tray.
3 Roast for around 15–20 minutes until just cooked and allow to rest for 5 minutes.
4 While the fish is resting, heat a stainless steel pan on a hot element. When hot, add the butter and move around the pan to melt evenly. Cook the butter until it takes on a rich brown colour and a toasty nutty aroma arises.
5 Remove from the heat and add the lemon juice to stop it cooking any further. Add the almonds and capers and lastly the parsley.
6 Season with salt and pepper and pour over the fish while still bubbling.

This is delicious with any whole baked fish and is best served with a crisp garden salad and boiled new-season potatoes.

Caper and lime butter sauce

1 In a saucepan, bring the wine and lime juice to a simmer.
2 Allow to reduce to around one-third, then add the cream.
3 Simmer gently and reduce by half.
4 Take from the heat and while whisking continuously drop in the butter. Whisk until butter has melted and the sauce is glossy and smooth.
5 Stir in capers and keep warm until ready to use.

'This summer has been especially long and given us lots of opportunities to use the deck and sit outside well into the evenings. So this beautifully presented and very delicious dish of Simon's has been a winner, and we all enjoy recommending it.'

serves four

Grilled Sole Fillet with Whitestone Rarebit & Niçoise

ingredients

- 16 large sole fillets
- butter
- seasoning

Rarebit

- 250 ml lager or beer
- 2 tbsp plain flour
- 2 tbsp Dijon mustard
- 300 g tasty cheese, grated
- 2 eggs
- 2 egg yolks

Niçoise salad

- 4 eggs, boiled for 6 minutes and cooled
- 200 g green bean batons, blanched and refreshed in cold water
- 16 anchovy fillets
- 16 new potatoes, cooked and cooled
- 100 g black Kalamata olives
- 4 tomatoes, chopped
- salad leaves to garnish
- house dressing (see appendix page 188)

method

1 In a heavy-bottomed pot, bring the beer to the boil.

2 Reduce heat and whisk in flour, avoiding lumps.

3 Add mustard and cheese and allow to melt slowly.

4 Move from the heat, allow to cool slightly, then beat in eggs and yolks until smooth. Cool completely.

5 To assemble, preheat a hot grill. Lay 4 fillets per serve on a greased tray and brush with melted butter. Grill for 4–5 minutes until three-quarters cooked. Cover with cooled rarebit and grill until browned and bubbling.

6 Arrange Niçoise ingredients attractively on serving plates for 4 people, and dress with house dressing.

7 Transfer hot sole fillets onto salad and serve immediately.

A globe artichoke ready for harvest in Alison McTavish's Moeraki garden.

'One of the "characters" of the Saturday morning Dunedin farmers' market is Colin Dennison of Evansdale Cheese near Waikouaiti – his theatrical voice cuts through the general hubbub to collar unwary customers as they stroll past his stall. Colin offers a fresh and salty cheese curd that makes this wonderful tart that comes from Yorkshire. It is flavoured with allspice and is great with a pot of tea for an afternoon treat.'

serves eight

Evansdale Fresh Curd Tart with Dried Blueberries

ingredients

Sweet pastry

250 g plain flour
pinch salt
75 g icing sugar
150 g cold butter, diced
1 lemon, zested
1 whole egg
1 egg yolk

Curd tart filling

125 g butter
60 g sugar
250 g curd cheese (replace with ricotta if unavailable)
125 g dried blueberries (currants can be used also)
1 tbsp breadcrumbs
pinch salt
1 tsp ground allspice
2 eggs, beaten

method

1. Preheat oven to 200 °C.
2. Combine dry ingredients in a large mixing bowl. Rub in butter to resemble fine breadcrumbs.
3. Add lemon zest and eggs and mix just to combine.
4. Wrap in cling film and rest in refrigerator for 30 minutes.
5. On a floured surface roll out pastry to cover a 25-cm tart tin.
6. Press in tin to remove air bubbles, prick the bottom with a fork and bake blind for 15 minutes.
7. To make the filling, cream butter and sugar together, and mix in the curd, blueberries and breadcrumbs.
8. Add the salt and spice and lastly the eggs and mix well.
9. Pour into the prebaked pastry case and bake for 20-30 minutes.
10. Allow to cool before serving.

'Years ago in Clyde I began my love affair with elderflowers and elderberries (along with wild thyme). Medieval folk admired them and their many uses have occupied me through all the seasons of the year. I think there should still be some elderberry wine in the cellar at Dunstan House – I can't imagine anyone would have been brave enough to drink it.'

Strawberries with Elderflower Sorbet

ingredients

Elderflower cordial

makes 1.5 litres

1 kg sugar
900 ml boiling water
40 g citric acid
15 large elderflower heads, freshly picked
2 lemons, sliced

Elderflower sorbet

makes 1 litre

600 ml elderflower cordial (as above)
400 ml water

method

Elderflower cordial

1 Dissolve the sugar with the boiling water in a large bowl and add the citric acid.
2 Providing they are insect-free, snip the flowers from the stalks of the elderflower and add to the sugar mixture with the sliced lemons. Cover with a clean cloth and refrigerate, stirring daily, for 5 days.
3 Strain through a fine sieve into sterilised bottles and store for up to a year in the refrigerator.

Elderflower sorbet

1 Combine the cordial and water and churn in an ice-cream machine, following the manufacturer's instructions. (Failing that, place in a tray and freeze, returning every hour to work through the ice crystals that form.)
2 Once fully frozen and grainy, place in a blender until fine and creamy.
3 Return to the freezer and leave for an hour before serving.

Serve with strawberries dusted with icing sugar.

‘Our sorbet selection is flavoured by the seasons. Wherever I walk, I see the next sorbet in the hedgerow or hanging in a tree.’ (Dessert chef Heather Wollaston)

makes 2.5 litres

Blackberry Sorbet

ingredients

1 kg blackberries

1 litre water

500 g caster sugar

method

1 Combine ingredients in a heavy-bottomed pot. Stir to dissolve, then gently bring to the boil.

2 Boil gently to soften the berries, remove from heat then purée and pass through a fine sieve.

3 Allow to cool, then churn in an ice-cream maker according to the manufacturer’s instructions.

makes 1 litre

Lemon Sorbet

ingredients

600 ml water

250 g caster sugar

1 lemon, zested

3 lemons, juiced

method

1 Dissolve the sugar in the water and bring gently to the boil.

2 Drop in the zest of one lemon and the juice of three.

3 Stir, allow to cool completely, then churn in an ice-cream maker according to the manufacturer’s instructions.

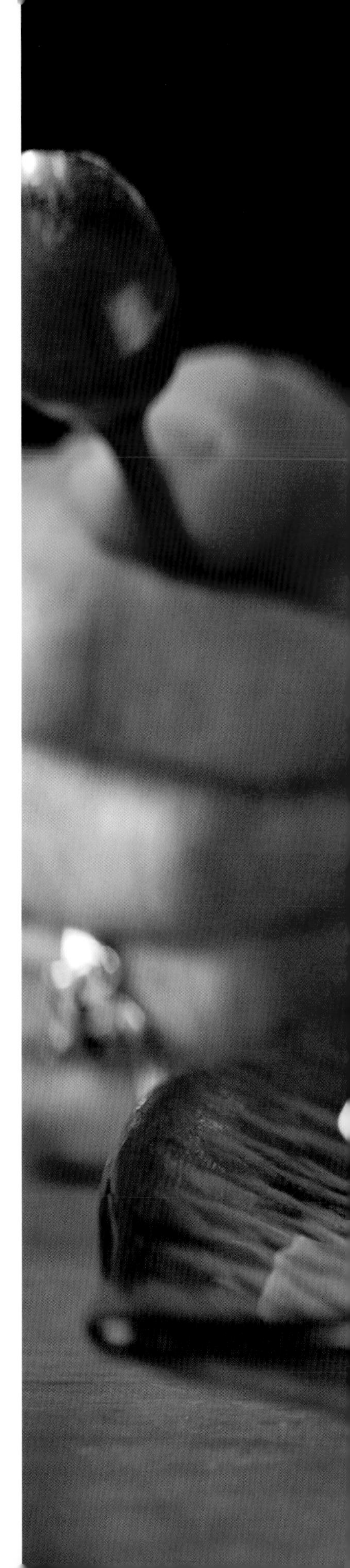

Senior chefs Kwon Pil Oh and Heather Wollaston at work in the restaurant with head chef Simon Peacock.

04/

summer

People having been living around Moeraki for hundreds of years, with prehistoric Maori exploiting the area for seasonal food camps (mahinga kai). Archaeologists have found evidence of moa-butchering sites at Shag Point and Waimataitai Lagoon near Katigi Point. In the eighteenth century, the war-like chief Taoka established a fortified pa on the Point, complete with defended pallisades and terraces for substantial wooden houses.

Pakeha arrived in 1836 when a shore whaling station was established in the curve of the bay at the present village – the first European settlement in North Otago. Two years later there began an influx of Maori from Kaikoura or Banks Peninsula that strengthened the settlement and provided wives for the whalers. When the whales ran out in the early 1840s, the whalers and their families took to farming. Land was set aside for Maori in 1848 around the present Second Kaik, but the kaik fell into disrepair and the Maori community moved to the outskirts of the Pakeha settlement around 1901.

As shipping expanded along the Otago coast, carrying wool, grain and Oamaru stone for building, Moeraki looked set to become a thriving commercial centre. Since the 1850s, the township had rivalled Oamaru as a cargo port and in the 1870s a new iron jetty was constructed and a harbour board appointed. The village also secured itself a stop on the main trunk railway as it was extended south from Oamaru and then on to Dunedin during the same decade.

But Moeraki's bid for greatness was not to last. A display board on the Millennium Walkway informs visitors that the instability of the land led to the

The Kotahitanga church sits quietly just off the road into the village.

closure of the short link line between the Hillgrove railhead and the anchorage in 1879 and ended Moeraki's chances of rivalling Oamaru as a port. Even today, the soft mudstone base on which the peninsula sits makes negotiating the access road a tricky affair.

However, the sea was to provide wealth of a different kind. Commercial fishing developed rapidly in the area in the 1890s, and by the turn of the century 38 boats and 72 fishermen were working out of the little harbour, with a fish-freezing factory on the wharf. Once again, Moeraki threatened to leave Oamaru behind. The catch could be quickly transported by rail to Oamaru and Dunedin and some smoking and curing was done on the spot. After the Second World War, shore facilities were gradually improved and, from the 1960s, the crayfish boom helped keep the industry on its feet.

However, commercial fishing has declined sharply over the past decade and only a handful of boats now operate out of the village. The small boats anchored in the bay are more likely to be used by recreational fishers, and for charters and wildlife tours. Moeraki is still a popular holiday centre, with cribs and a motor camp catering for the pleasure-seekers who swell the permanent population of 90 or so each summer. And, of course, Fleurs Place is perhaps the biggest drawcard of all.

A wildlife haven

Moeraki is a paradise for wildlife, and there can't be another restaurant in the country where you can dine in the company of so many native birds and marine mammals. From the tables on the balcony, you look across to the old iron jetty crowded with shags, black-backed gulls and white-fronted terns, and below the fisherman's wharf on the other side of the bay mollymawks and petrels fight over fish scraps whenever a boat ties up. Raiding parties of red-billed gulls dive in to clean up any al fresco leftovers. Fur seals haul out on the rocks below the restaurant, and a big sea lion turns on a regular performance in the bay. To cap it all, every evening rafts of little blue penguins come ashore to find their nests right on Fleur's doorstep.

Further along the coast, Maukiekie Island just offshore from First Kaik is topped with packed nesting colonies of three shag species – little, spotted and Stewart Island – and was the first place in Otago to record breeding by elegant royal spoonbills in 1984. And the wildlife sanctuary at Katigi Point, at the southern extremity of the peninsula, is famous for its fur seals – snoozing or scrapping in the rock pools, or lolling about in the ocean below steep cliffs. The rare yellow-eyed penguins that come ashore here from late afternoon are surprisingly approachable. They seem to know that humans will not step beyond the wire fencing that runs along the headland and forms a flimsy barrier between the two species.

Marama Higgins – Local identity

Marama Higgins must have the best view in Moeraki. The big windows of her hillside house take in the full sweep of the bay, with its flotilla of small boats resting at anchor, an arc of misty hills beyond. She makes an elegant figure sitting in her airy living room, surrounded by solid but comfortable

A fur seal at Katigi Point warns visitors to keep their distance.

furnishings and portraits of her family. Now 80, Marama was born in Moeraki and has lived here 'on and off' all her life. Although her career as a schoolteacher took her all around the country, she managed to do a stint at the local school before it closed in 1989.

Marama is proud to be still living on the family property. Her mother was a Hampstead and her father a Leonard – both old Moeraki names. While Maori cultural life has declined over the years here, there is still a substantial Maori presence in the village. There is a meeting of the runanga once a month on the marae and an Anglican priest comes over from Waikouaiti to take regular services in the Kotahitanga church. (One of its stained-glass windows depicts the leader of the Maori community in the nineteenth century, Matiaha Tiramorehu.) And people who have left the village come back to celebrate special events such as the hui-a-tau or annual meeting of Ngai Tahu, which was held on the marae in 2006 – with 1000 guests.

For Marama, Fleur's arrival has been a real fillip for the village. 'It's lovely to have her here,' she says. 'She's good fun. She brings the people into Moeraki. If any cars come up this way, you can be sure they're heading for Fleur's.'

Heather and Fleur with their pickings from Bob and Lesley's garden. **Opposite page:** Long-term resident Marama Higgins.

Summer fruits from a Hampden garden

In one of those serendipitous meetings so typical of Moeraki, Fleur met charter-boat operators Bob Williams and Lesley Hale down at the wharf as they were preparing to set off on a fishing cruise. She quickly discovered that they had a back yard full of berry fruit and that they were more than happy to give her access to it. Enough said.

On a sunny January day, Fleur and dessert chef Heather Wollaston joined Lesley in picking two large basins full of succulent blackcurrants and an armful of rhubarb. Boysenberries and blackberries also grow abundantly in this Hampden garden – Lesley says that 9 kg of currants can easily be picked from just a single bush. She adds that the soil is treated with nothing more elaborate than a side dressing of general garden fertiliser every winter.

This afternoon's haul will shortly become part of this evening's iced blackcurrant parfait, and may even find its way into a fruit crumble or two …

Mick the egg man

Mick Gallavin has been a local identity for around 20 years, raising pigs for trophy hunters on his rambling property just out of Hampden. Although Mick's thriving collection of Captain Cookers is his main claim to fame, he also supplies Fleur with a constant flow of free-range eggs – up to 20 trays a week in the whitebait season for the restaurant's very popular whitebait omelettes.

Mick's property is swarming with chickens, geese and Muscovy ducks (duck eggs is a developing line) and he collects his eggs from under hedges, in old sheds and underneath abandoned car bodies – wherever his hens choose to lay. Mick's hens are definitely not purebred, and he regularly rescues birds which have spent their lives in cages on battery farms. 'The poor buggers don't even know how to walk when I get them,' he says. Nevertheless, they thrive in their new home and certainly produce the goods: 'Simon couldn't work out why his sponges were so yellow when he first started using my eggs.'

Mick's regular trips to the restaurant serve another purpose, too – he goes home with a truckload of kitchen scraps to feed up his prize porkers.

Muscovy ducks roam with free-range hens on Mick Gallavin's Hampden property.

summer recipes

'Wild fennel can be picked all through North Otago, both inland and on the coast. The stalks can be dried to burn for the fish-smoking process, and the seeds make a great tea infusion.'

Beetroot-cured Salmon Gravadlax with Fennel Vodka

ingredients

Simon's fennel vodka

1 bottle vodka
1 large handful of wild fennel

Salmon gravadlax

1 whole salmon, filleted in two and pin-boned, leaving the skin on
3 lemons
375 g sea salt
355 g sugar
black peppercorns, juniper berries, chopped fennel
25 ml fennel vodka
1 raw beetroot, grated

method

Simon's fennel vodka

1 Take a double shot of vodka from the bottle to brace yourself and venture out to gather wild fennel from the neighbour's garden.
2 Return and wash the fennel - and cram as much into the bottle of vodka as possible.
3 Store in the freezer and leave for a month before drinking.

Salmon gravadlax

1 Lay the two fillets of salmon side by side on a plastic tray.
2 Zest the lemons and squeeze the juice and combine with remaining ingredients except the beetroot.
3 Cake the mixture onto one of the fillets and sandwich with the other fillet.
4 Wrap tightly with cling film and weigh down lightly with a ceramic dish.
5 Refrigerate for 24–36 hours. You will notice a lot of liquid drawing from the salmon fillets.
6 Wash in cold water, discard juice and remaining herbs, etc., and gently pat dry.
7 Cover the salmon fillets with the grated beetroot and wrap again in cling film. Leave for further 12–24 hours.
8 Again wash and pat dry.
9 Slice thinly on an angle, cutting towards the skin and off it.

Serve with a shot of the fennel vodka on the side, some toasted rye bread and a little cream cheese mixed with horseradish.

'I tie my bull kelp up to the wharf to keep it fresh, and just cut off what we need. After a big storm, there's always a lot of it lying on the beaches and then it's easy to gather.'

serves two

Bull Kelp with Clams & Mussels

ingredients

- piece of fresh bull kelp, dark green, cut from the thick end and around 30–45 cm long
- 1 dozen mussels, scraped and debearded
- 2 dozen clams, washed
- 2 tbsp butter
- 1 lemon, quartered

method

1 Wash the kelp and ensure it is free from grit and sand. Create a pocket by carefully slicing along the fibrous middle of the kelp. Take care not to puncture, and check for nicks and cuts.

2 Cut through until around 2 cm from the end. Stuff the cavity with the shellfish, butter and the lemon wedges.

3 Using a metal skewer, fold over the edge of the kelp and sew together to create an enclosed parcel.

4 Roast in the oven for around 20 minutes or over an open fire until bloated from the internal steam and the shellfish open inside.

Kaimoana Platter – Food from the Sea

Our kaimoana platter is one of the most popular dishes on the menu. Producing one 'kai' would be an awful mission – but turning out dozens of them is such fun.

Each day, a fresh haul of the sea's delicacies is added to the smoking process and each catch is surveyed with the kai platter in mind. Fish frames, wings, livers, eels and mussels are steeped in brine and dried before going into the smoker along with manuka woodchips, fennel stalks, bay leaves and wilted herbs from the kitchen.

Freshly filleted blue cod is marinated in lemon and lime juice and later dressed with coconut cream, coriander and chilli. The escabeche – literally, 'pickled fish' – sitting in the chiller in large oblong dishes, and the shellfish, mussels, cockles and queen scallops – scraped and cleaned in their own containers – await their turn to be added to the mix.

Sue arrives at work each morning armed with an array of hedgerow clippings, wild herbs, ferns and flowers to garnish the kai platters – first running her prized selection past Fleur to ensure nothing gathered is poisonous!

ingredients

Escabeche

1 part white wine
1 part white wine vinegar
1 part water
bay leaves
peppercorns
onions, sliced
lemons, sliced
pinch of saffron
salt
sugar

Escabeche

method

1 Prepare a court bouillon by bringing equal amounts of white wine, white wine vinegar and water to the boil. Add fresh bay leaves, peppercorns, onions, lemons and saffron.

2 Season with salt and sugar and pour hot over prepared fish fillets with skin on. Allow to marinate overnight in the fridge.

'My father and brother were deerstalkers, so venison has featured on the table throughout my life. Dad and Gerard's back steaks and hindquarters had to be dragged a long way back to the car – there were no four-wheel drives or helicopters around in those days, so the venison was usually covered in tussock and twigs by the time it got home. Depending on the length of time they were away, it could also be a bit green and maggoty – but always hung well.'

serves twelve

Smoked Venison with Horopito, Honey & Mustard

ingredients

- 500 g brown sugar
- 500 g rock salt
- 2 tsp saltpetre (optional)
- 3 x 500-g pieces of venison from the Denver leg, all sinews and silverskin removed
- 200 ml runny manuka honey
- 150 g wholegrain mustard
- 3 tbsp dried horopito leaves, crushed
- 1 tbsp black peppercorns, crushed

method

1 Mix together brown sugar and salts and spread out on a stainless steel, non-reactive oven tray.

2 Coat the venison in the sugar and salt and leave to stand for 1–1½ hours.

3 When liquids have drawn from the venison, wash the pieces in fresh water removing all salt traces. Pat dry.

4 Mix together remaining ingredients and coat dried venison in the mix. Leave to stand 24 hours.

5 Smoke the meat over a low heat allowing it to dry slightly, leaving it still rare and pink in the centre (about 2 hours).

Serve in a salad with pickled beetroot, fresh seasonal greens, a wedge of your favourite blue cheese and a handful of toasted walnuts.

'It's a rare and special thing to be able to serve a fresh, whole baked fish – any fish – in a restaurant on a daily basis. I never cease to be amazed that I'm able to do this.'

serves one

Whole Baked Flounder

ingredients

1 whole fresh flounder per person, washed with sea water
cooking spray or vegetable oil

Tartare sauce

makes 2 cups

2 free-range egg yolks
½ tsp salt
1 tsp Dijon mustard
2 tsp white wine vinegar
1 cup vegetable or soya bean oil
2 tsp chopped spring onions
1 tsp chopped capers
2 tsp chopped gherkins
1 tsp chopped parsley

method

1 Preheat the oven to 190 °C.
2 Grease an oven tray with the oil and place the flounder on this.
3 Roast for 8–10 minutes, depending on size, or until the skin can just be pulled away from the flesh.
4 Allow it to rest for 2–3 minutes.

Serve with tartare sauce, plenty of lemons and a fresh garden salad or steamed seasonal vegetables on the side.

Tartare sauce

1 In a large, heavy mixing bowl, place the yolks with the salt, mustard and vinegar.
2 Whilst whisking, slowly pour in the oil drop by drop until the mixture begins to thicken. Continue with the oil until the mixture is pale and thick.
3 Add the remaining chopped flavourings and taste for seasoning.

'A lot of egg whites are left over from making our brûlées – so we ease our conscience by making the odd pavlova.'

Makes one large pavlova mounded in the centre or eight individual-serve quenelles

Pavlova with Hedgerow Blackberries

ingredients

Pavlova

4 egg whites
pinch salt
250 g caster sugar
1 tsp white wine vinegar
2 tsp cornflour
1 tsp vanilla essence or the scraped seeds from one vanilla pod

Blackberry compote

200 g caster sugar
75 ml water (not necessary if using frozen berries)
squeeze of lemon juice
scraped vanilla pod from the pavlova
500 g fresh, clean hedgerow blackberries (you can use your frozen stash in the off season)

method

1 Preheat oven to 180 °C.
2 In a clean metal bowl or electric mixer, whisk the egg whites with the salt until firm peaks are reached.
3 While still whisking, slowly add the sugar until very firm and satiny.
4 Fold through the vinegar, cornflour and vanilla and shape onto greaseproof paper.
5 Place in oven and reduce heat to 140 °C. Cook for 30–45 minutes depending on size, then turn off heat and allow to cool overnight in the oven.
6 To make the compote, warm the sugar, water, lemon and vanilla together to create a sugar syrup.
7 When boiling, drop in blackberries and allow to cool. (If using frozen berries, thaw, reserve the juice and use this to make the sugar syrup.)

To assemble

8 Spoon compote over pavlova and drizzle with the syrup, then finish with soft whipped cream.

'These custard pots are fantastic served just as they are – or enhanced with the addition of Bob's hedgerow blackberries or Nathan's organic strawberries. Garnish with homemade almond bread and half a banana passionfruit from Joy's garden across the road.'

serves eight

Crème Brûlée

ingredients

1 vanilla pod

1 litre cream

12 egg yolks

250 g caster sugar

method

1 Split and scrape the seeds from a vanilla pod and add to a litre of cream.

2 Bring to the boil slowly and pour hot over the egg yolks and caster sugar.

3 Pour the custard into serving pots and cook covered in a water bath in a low oven (110 °C) for 40 minutes - or until the custard wobbles slightly - and allow to cool.

4 Spread a teaspoon of caster sugar over the top and caramelise using a blow torch - taking care not to set the kitchen on fire!

'This dish gives me every excuse to buy those wonderful crystal parfait glasses languishing in Salvation Army op shops – along with the long parfait spoons still in their "21st birthday present" satin-lined boxes.'

serves eight

Iced Blackcurrant Parfait

ingredients

- 1 cup sugar
- 350 g blackcurrants, fresh or frozen
- 4 egg yolks
- 1½ gelatine leaves
- 2 tbsp cold water
- 250 ml cream, softly whipped
- 2 tsp crème de cassis

method

1 In a heavy-bottomed pot, dissolve the sugar in the blackcurrants before bringing to the boil. Cook for 2 minutes.
2 Purée and pass through a fine sieve.
3 Whisk egg yolks until pale and creamy. Pour on hot blackcurrant purée and whisk to a stiff mousse.
4 Soften gelatine in the cold water. Warm gently to dissolve and add this to the blackcurrant mousse.
5 Gently fold the mousse through the softly whipped cream and crème de cassis.
6 Divide into eight lightly oiled pudding moulds and freeze until ready to serve.

Serve these turned out with more whipped cream and a drizzle of crème de cassis.

'Heather makes the most wonderful Victorian desserts – each one traditional and perfect. It's such fun collecting the seasonal produce for her to use. I planted a gooseberry bush at the back door of Fleurs Place that reminds me of my Mum and Dad. It doesn't produce enough fruit yet to make this gooseberry fool – but it has provided the garnish.'

serves six

Gooseberry Fool

ingredients

The fruit

500 g frozen gooseberries
250 g caster sugar
100 ml elderflower cordial (see page 145)

The custard

250 ml milk
125 ml cream
1 split vanilla pod, or 1 tsp vanilla essence
5 egg yolks
50 g caster sugar

The cream

1 litre softly whipped cream

method

1 Heat a heavy-bottomed pot on the stove-top. Rumble frozen gooseberries with sugar and pour directly into the hot pan.
2 Stir rapidly until the liquid leaves the gooseberries and a syrup is formed.
3 Add the cordial and simmer until gooseberries begin to burst. The compote should be quite thick and still quite tart.
4 Allow to cool completely.
5 To make the custard, bring the milk and cream with the vanilla to just below boiling point in a heavy-bottomed pot.
6 Whisk together the egg yolks and sugar and pour the hot cream mixture over this while stirring.
7 Return the mix back to a low heat and stir continuously until it begins to thicken and will coat the back of a spoon (do not allow to boil or it will become grainy and curdled).
8 Strain through a fine sieve and set the bowl on ice to cool quickly. Allow to cool completely.
9 Make sure every aspect of the dish is thoroughly chilled, then mix half of the fruit compote through the whipped cream and swirl through half the custard. Do not overmix.
10 Build individual serving glasses by starting with the remaining fruit, then adding a layer of custard and topping with the cream and fruit mix. Repeat this procedure until the glasses are full.

Serve with shortbreads on the side.

A fool needn't be too technical. Its beauty lies in the contrast of (almost) too-tart fruit, swirled through rich custard and lightened with cream – it is the very essence of enjoying seasonal fruit. This dish is also wonderful with rhubarb, hedgerow berries or even banana passionfruit.

'This is another great way of using up surplus egg whites, and we serve it with anything from coffee to custards.' (Head chef Simon Peacock)

Old-fashioned Almond Bread

ingredients

3 egg whites
90 g caster sugar
90 g plain flour
90 g unblanched almonds

method

1 Preheat oven to 180 °C.
2 Whip the egg whites until thick, beat in the sugar then fold gently through the flour and almonds.
3 Pour into a well-oiled loaf tin and bake for 30–40 minutes or until firm to the touch.
4 Cool turned out on a wire rack. When cold, slice thinly with a serrated knife.
5 Spread out on baking trays, lower the oven temperature to 140 °C and bake for 20 minutes until pale gold and crisp.

makes 750 ml

House Dressing

ingredients

- 200 ml white wine vinegar
- 2 tbsp wholegrain mustard
- 2 tbsp local honey
- 1 tbsp strong Dijon mustard
- 500 ml vegetable oil or light olive oil
- seasoning

method

In a bowl, whisk together the vinegar, mustards and honey. Drizzle in oil while whisking.

Season and keep in a bottle in the fridge.

Glossary

horopito	pepper tree
hui	meeting, gathering
kaika, kainga	village, settlement
kaimoana	seafood
karengo	edible seaweed related to Japanese nori
kaumatua	elder
koura	freshwater crayfish
kumara	sweet potato
mahinga kai	seasonal food-gathering or camps
manuka	tea-tree
marae	village meeting area
pa	stockaded village
pawhero	variety of potato
puha	sow-thistle
rewena bread	a traditional bread made with potatoes
runanga	council, assembly
titi	muttonbird
urupa	cemetery, burial ground

List of Suppliers

Mean Greens
23 Kenilworth Road, Oamaru
Phone: (03) 437 1012
Mobile: 027 547 3367

Evansdale Cheese
1 RD Waikouaiti
Phone: (03) 465 8101
Email: info@evansdalecheese.co.nz
www.evansdalecheese.co.nz

Joe's Vegie Market
11-15 Ribble Street, Oamaru
Phone: (03) 433 1126

Kaan's Catering Supplies Ltd.
29 Willis Street, Dunedin
Phone: (03) 477 7121
Mobile: 027 433 9155
Freephone: 0800 777 121

Southern Clams Ltd.
PO Box 483, Dunedin
Phone: (03) 477 1505
Freephone: 0800 771 505
www.nzclams.com

Kakanui Produce
C/o Postal Delivery Centre, Kakanui
Phone: (03) 439 5153
Mobile: 021 114 0613
Email: vivscott@xtra.co.nz

Whitestone Cheese Ltd.
3 Torridge Street, Oamaru
Phone: (03) 434 8098
Mobile: 021 439 533
www.whitestonecheese.co.nz

Rod Phillip Asparagus
Phone: (03) 465 1278
Mobile: 027 275 6776

Pasta D'Oro Ltd.
616 Kaikorai Valley Road
PO Box 394, Dunedin
Phone: (03) 488 5371

Aroha Organics
Steph and Nathan Davis
Main South Road, St Andrews
Phone: (03) 612 6092

Fenland Organics
Bob Burton
11 Lancaster Street, Hampden
Phone: (03) 439 4488

The Strictly Coffee Company
23 Bath Street, Dunedin
Phone: (03) 479 0017

Oast House Liquorland
261 Thames Street, Oamaru
Phone: (03) 434 9883
Fax: (03) 434 9908

Blue Water Products
PO Box 2135, Dunedin
Phone: (03) 477 7044
Fax: (03) 477 7202

NZ Eel Processing
PO Box 43, Te Kauwhata
Phone: (07) 826 3616

Campbell's Butchery
160 Thames Street, Oamaru
Phone: (03) 434 8780

Hairy Mussel Company
Crail Bay, RD 2, Picton Sounds
Phone: (03) 579 8231

Heart of the Desert Saffron
12 Minors Terrace, RD 2, Cromwell
Phone: (03) 445 1909
Email: saffron@xtra.co.nz

Mt Cook Salmon Ltd.
PO Box 67, Twizel 7944
Phone: (03) 435 0085
Mobile: 021 370 038

Harbour Fish Ltd.
PO Box 15, Port Chalmers
Dunedin

Service Foods (DN) Ltd.
9 Timaru Street
PO Box 2377, Dunedin
Phone: (03) 455 2668
Fax: (03) 455 2996

Sanford Ltd.
(fresh seafood supplies)
Hall Street
Pvt. Bag, Timaru
Phone: (03) 688 0354

Talley's Nelson
(fresh seafood supplies)
PO Box 7064, Nelson
Phone: (03) 548 0109

Recipe Index